LIVERPOOL

An unchanging land and sea scape: sand dunes and the Irish Sea near the mouth of the River Mersey. In the early days of the town's history, the dunes extended southwards almost to the present-day Pier Head. AUTHOR

LIVERPOOL
The making of the City on the Mersey

PETER KENNERLEY

For Jim Craig
and all my friends on the staff of
Saint Margaret of Antioch School,
founded 1888 and closed 2010
because they thought it was too small.
"This is a good school
which serves its community well
and is highly valued by
pupils and parents."
Ofsted Report

Copyright © Peter Kennerley, 2010

First edition, 2010

Published by Palatine Books,
an imprint of Carnegie Publishing Ltd
Carnegie House,
Chatsworth Road,
Lancaster, LA1 4SL
www.carnegiepublishing.com

ISBN 978-1-874181-69-9

Designed and typeset by Carnegie Book Production
Printed and bound in the UK by Information Press, Oxford

Contents

'Another Place': an Antony Gormley figure looking out across the Mersey estuary from the shore at Crosby.

ONE

On the shore

I MUST ADMIT that I have not the slightest glimmer of a memory of my first arrival in Liverpool. I was eighteen months old at the time, and when the removal men found it impossible to accommodate my large black pram in their tightly packed van my mother pushed pram and first-born through Birkenhead, on to a ferry, along the Dock Road, up to the Dingle and along Aigburth Road to Aigburth Vale.

Almost two-thirds of a century later, in glorious late summer weather, I was walking past the famous cast-iron church of St Michael in the Hamlet, and I had the clearest vision of myself as a child. I had attended St Michael's school – as had my parents – and at the age of eleven I won what was regarded as a prestigious school prize. I clearly remember the teacher apologising that she had been unable to find a history of Liverpool as requested and that, instead, she had bought a big thick book with a dark green cover called *The Home of Mankind*.

I never did read that book, and I would much rather have been given a history of the locality where I lived. I continued to be fascinated by such features as the fragment of sandstone ruin on the golf links; the little stream that bubbled out of the ground near by; and the great smooth blocks of red sandstone down on the shore, Jericho Farm. Even more interesting were my father's occasional stories about his grandfather's cottage just above the shoreline at Jericho – we sometimes walked there very early on a Sunday morning – and about the little boat from which my fishermen forebears had made their livings before the Manchester Ship Canal or Garston Docks were built, and before pollution had rendered the muddy waters of the Mersey smelly and lifeless.

This is the Kennerley ancestral home, Fisherman's Cottage, which was situated near the bottom of Jericho Lane on a site now completely covered by the Otterspool Promenade.

On a particularly pleasant morning several months ago, I walked the full length of Otterspool promenade. This had not existed during my early child-hood, and indeed thousands of tons of city refuse had been dumped in order to cover up the clay cliffs, cast-iron shore and golf links of my childhood play. Flats and houses now cover Jericho Farm house and fields. I became quite maudlin as I thought of all that had gone as I leaned on the railings watching the sun shimmering on the tide and the gulls gliding effortlessly against a cloudless sky.

In the channel that runs towards Garston Docks, close to the Liverpool shore, I saw a large black bird bobbing on the water. Suddenly it dived and reap-peared some distance away. This it did three times before flapping its slightly ungainly wings and flying off low across the water towards the Cheshire shore. It was a cormorant. At the Pier Head two further cormorants were visible: larger-than-life, copper sculptures on the twin towers of the Liver Building. Central to the official crest of the city, these fabled birds were cormorants (although the original crest of King John had actually featured an eagle).

The appearance of that real bird fishing in the Mersey, within a stone's throw of my family's ancestral Fisherman's Cottage and only a quarter of a mile from my present house was the immediate catalyst for the writing of this book. I knew at once that the river and the ever-changing Mersey shore were going to be close to the heart of the piece, and I also had a good idea about the nature of the work I wanted to produce. This would not be a book for academic histo-rians. Rather, I would be writing for that inquisitive 11-year-old who had wanted a history of Liverpool as a school prize; for ordinary Liverpudlians and visitors to the city after the eight hundredth celebration of the first charter in 1207 and the European Capital of Culture in 2008.

The task of writing was made harder by Liverpool's habit of knocking down or covering up much evidence of the past. We all have little stories of personal loss, be it the Goree Piazzas, the Customs House, row upon row of terraced communities. I well remember my mild and deeply charitable mother telling me about a meeting in the Church Hall of St Andrew's, Aigburth Road. 'The Bishop was there,' she said, 'and he had a piece of my fruit cake and said it was beautiful. After that the bugger said he was closing the church!' Now there is only a block of flats and the memories of all my choirboy childhood. Yet for over 500 years Liverpool had a castle; there was a royal deer park; the Old Dock was the first of its kind in the world; and the Overhead Railway was a wonder of the age.

Liverpool's history is fascinating for many reasons. The obvious starting point is its status as Britain's greatest port city (other ports might have rivalled or even exceeded Liverpool in some ways at some times, but none could match Liverpool's specialisation in all things maritime). Sailors, emigrants, immigrants and migrant workers all contributed to provide Liverpool with a social mix of peoples that was more rich and diverse than that found almost anywhere else (bar London, perhaps). For all but the last thirty years Liverpool lay firmly within Lancashire, yet it is hardly typical of the county, whose accent ends

Ferry across the Mersey. In my childhood thousands of people from the Wirral crossed the river every day in one of the little fleet of Mersey ferries. Today they operate mini river cruises.

AUTHOR

One of the famous Liver Birds, large copper figures, which are securely anchored at the top of the ornate twin towers of the Liver Building. The clock face is the largest of its kind in the country.
AUTHOR

Speke Hall is one of the oldest and best-known buildings in the area, although Speke itself did not become part of Liverpool until the twentieth century. The hall is a fine example of a Tudor half-timbered house, built by members of the Norris family in the sixteenth century, and largely unaltered to this day.
AUTHOR

The Mersey with the Wirral in the distance viewed from Otterspool Park, which in my early childhood was one vast rubbish tip. It is now a splendid recreational area with riverside walkways. It is now possible to walk from Pier Head almost to Garston without moving away from the river.

AUTHOR

Some of the famous Pier Head buildings silhouetted against the setting sun. Unfortunately, this view is no longer possible because of new buildings.

AUTHOR

Cormorants perch on the dock side with a good view over to new riverside houses, flats and the two cathedrals. The waters of the docks are clean enough for the swimming leg of triathlon events and are the base for large numbers of recreational vessels.

abruptly somewhere between Ormskirk and Maghull. For many centuries Liverpool looked not inland, but outwards: one reason why 'The World in One City' was so appropriate an epithet.

Liverpool's renowned spirit and vitality come not only from its maritime past or its historic cosmopolitanism; in part it derives also from deep divisions and contrasts that have always existed here – between social classes; between the rich and the very poor; between religions and, by association, in politics too.

At the very heart of the story has always flowed the river. Where its waters touched the city, it represented a boundary with the wider world possessed of a distinctive frontier spirit; a gateway to lands and fabulous wealth overseas; a point of departure and of return; a living presence made all the more immediate because the city is built on a long, low prominence from which the Mersey can be seen to full advantage from many points. Other cities turn their backs on the rivers that run through their hearts: the Mersey is such a dominant geographical and emotional feature that such denial or concealment are not possible here. In Liverpool the river is the heart.

This book is a personal journey – a pilgrimage if you like – through the story of the most remarkable city I know. This is my city as I see it; it is very much my story. If you know Liverpool well, I hope that it offers some new perspectives on which to ponder; and I certainly expect it to remind you of some of the people and places that have shaped the way the city is today. If you are a visitor or a newcomer to Liverpool, I trust that it will give you an insight into just why so many people develop such an abiding love for their native city.

I was asked to write a short, readable account of eight hundred years of Liverpool history: no easy task. I decided to handle the basic narrative in a series of short chapters arranged chronologically. To have expanded upon the lives of significant inhabitants or details of buildings and localities would have distorted the narrative line and yet they would have to be an essential part of any book, however short. To use the terminology of the photographer, I have inserted a series of self-contained units called Portraits or Landscapes which can be read independently of the surrounding narrative. Fot all that I have omitted, I can only apologise.

The statue of Peter Pan in Sefton Park was a gift to the children of Liverpool in 1928. After careful restoration by National Museums Liverpool, it was returned to the park in 2005, where it has delighted generations of children.
AUTHOR

Sandstone ridges are the dominant geological features that run north to south through Liverpool and district. Little of the rock is now visible, being covered with dense buildings, but this photograph taken on Thurstaston Hill on the Wirral gives some impression of what the Liverpool ridges must have been like once.

'The history of Liverpool is a blank'

HE EARLIEST existing reference to what we now know as
Liverpool was in a document of 1191. It is possible that there was a
handful of settlers living in primitive conditions at the time, but no
proof of this has yet been unearthed. In fact, one of the classic histories of
Liverpool sums it up in its very first sentence: 'Before the end of the eleventh
century the history of Liverpool is a blank'.

Before the foundation of the town of Liverpool by King John in 1207 the area
was unremarkable, similar in character to much of the neighbouring coastline.
As R.W. Cowell put it, '... the landscape pattern for approximately 9,000 years
before the Domesday Survey was rooted in woodland, fen, swamp, peat bog,
and long sweeps of coast'.

The River Mersey is quite a short river, yet remarkable in its appearance as
it flows towards the sea, widening out to three miles before bending northwards
into a mile-wide mouth scoured by fast-flowing tides. Importantly, a small tidal
creek or inlet known as the Pool used to flow into this narrower part of the river.
About half a mile long, the Pool gave Liverpool part of its name; the 'liver'
element probably meant 'muddy' or 'sluggish'. It was around this sluggish tidal
inlet that the new town of Liverpool was to grow.

There used to be sandy beaches and sandhills to the north of what is now the
Pier Head. Much of the ground was heavy boulder clay and deposits of river
silt, while further inland the ground rose quite steeply to sandstone ridges up
to two hundred feet in height, covered with heather and gorse. Nearer to the
river there would have been dense natural woodland. At the top of what we

know as Brownlow Hill was a marshy area, later known as the Moss Lake, which drained into the Pool near the bottom of what was later to become William Brown Street.

There is evidence of some Stone Age presence in the region, maybe 3,000 years ago, revealed by the Calder Stones which mark an ancient burial place. Some flint arrow heads and earthenware jars containing cremated bones from a similar period were unearthed in 1867 on Olive Mount in Wavertree. It used to be thought that there was no evidence of Roman occupation of the region, but excavation for sewers uncovered a section of stone pavement near to St Mary's Church, Grassendale, in 1855 two years after a similar find at Otterspool.

Place-names provide evidence of both Anglo-Saxon and Danish settlement. Toxteth, Walton, Everton and Bootle are of Saxon origin; and Kirkdale, West Derby, Crosby, Roby and Thingwall are Danish in origin. Thing Wald means hill of counsel, a place of importance; Mackerfield means the field of slaughter commemorating King Penda of Mercia's victory over King Oswald in 642. In the eleventh century Edward the Confessor held the manor at West Derby.

The Domesday Book of 1086 does not mention Liverpool itself, despite its references to Crosby, Litherland, Bootle, Walton, Kirkdale, Smithdown, Wavertree and Toxteth, each of which might well not have signified anything more extensive than single farms or small hamlets. Chester was the only established town in the whole of the Mersey basin. The only significant settlement near the site of later Liverpool was West Derby, known to most modern inhabitants as the destination on the front of a bus.

At the time of the Domesday Book the whole of south-west Lancashire was a desolate area. The estimated population in the whole sweep of land between the Ribble and the Mersey was remarkably low, at just two people per square mile. The 'hundred' of West Derby stretched from Southport to Hale and east to Wigan, and the total population was no more than 3,000. Professor Ramsey Muir wrote, 'In Western Europe there were few more remote and isolated corners'.

In the shadow of St Mary's Church, West Derby, there is an imposing nineteenth-century sandstone building, an open grassed area called Castle Green and rows of twentieth-century semi-detached houses. No ruined walls remain, but there was certainly an Anglo Saxon wooden fort on this site superseded by a stone-built motte-and-bailey Norman castle. The manor of West Derby was central to the lives of all the people, and they each owed allegiance to their feudal lord, on whose land they were forced to work for a set number of days each year. This lord had considerable control over their lives, and the

The Mersey shore on the Liverpool side of the river is now entirely man-made, but this photograph of the river and shore-line near Eastham on the Wirral gives the twenty-first-century viewer some idea of what parts of the Toxteth shore must have been like for centuries before industrialisation.
AUTHOR

common people belonged to the land and could not leave it; all legal matters for the whole region were settled at the hundred court in West Derby. There were no made roads in the region and the people had to walk from Liverpool along a track which years later was to become Dale Street and London Road.

The phenomenal success and growth of Liverpool in the nineteenth century gave rise to such a series of massive buildings that the natural contours of the land have been lost, and we must try to remove them from the mind's eye in order to visualise the original topography as well as the nature and, above all, the very small scale of what was the early medieval borough. As we shall see in later chapters the town of Liverpool really has two histories: a rather quiet, fairly undistinguished early history consisting of small-town living, followed by an amazing, radical history of trade, shipping and enormous demographic change and growth.

In an attempt to glimpse Liverpool's early history, and to peel away some 800 years of urban development – to see what King John's advisors saw as they travelled south through Lancashire in 1206 – I decided to supplement my academic researches by walking around the streets of Liverpool. And, as it is

The dunes and the Irish Sea no more than half a mile from Seaforth Docks and Liverpool Freeport. The vessel on the horizon speaks of today; the rest of the view is timeless.
AUTHOR

one of the oldest features on the famous Pier Head landscape, the tower of Liverpool Parish Church (the present one dates from 1815) seemed to offer a suitable vantage point for observation. From old maps and pictures I knew that the original shoreline had been hard up to the churchyard wall in front of the church, yet the modern shoreline is some distance away. How could this be? The painful ascent of the spiral steps to the ringing chamber, past the bell chamber and out onto the tower roof below the lantern was worth the effort, and yet disappointing. At one time the tower of St Nick's would have provided a superb view, but now I felt dwarfed by the modern buildings towering over me, and especially by the twin towers of the famous Liver Building. It was much easier to ascend to the roof of this building, as a lift delivered me effortlessly in no time at all. Looking to north and south, from Seaforth to Garston, the extent of man-made Liverpool at once became obvious.

It is one of the most remarkable facts about Liverpool's topography that all of the Liverpool docks, bar one, and all of the broad strip of land between St

Nicholas' church and where the river is now – including the land occupied by the Liver Building and the other Pierhead buildings – are built on reclaimed land. Successive engineers had built the retaining walls of their docks out into the river rather than excavating them from from dry land; this meant that the river itself was narrowed by up to one-third, and that the original shoreline is now not at all obvious from ground level.

The bed of the original tidal creek – the Pool, from which the settlement had taken its name – has also gone. The first stage in its demise was the construction, some 300 years ago, of the very first dock; for ease of construction this was sited right in the middle of the Pool itself. Land behind was back-filled and a custom house was built at its head. Fortunately, old maps and records enable us to trace the old Pool to the foot of William Brown Street. The half-mile flow of the Pool formed a roughly triangular peninsula which was to become the site of the little borough.

Map over which has been printed the original shoreline and the tidal inlet that gave Liverpool its name.

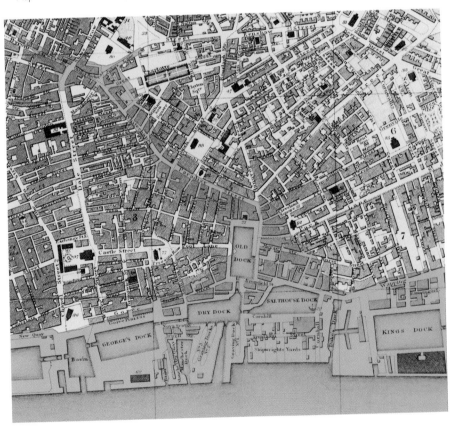

THE RIVER MERSEY

A friend tried to catch me out recently by asking, 'Which is the closest professional football ground to the Mersey?' Without delay I was able to reply, 'Stockport County'. Not that I am at all knowledgeable about football, but I had just spent a whole day trying to find one of the sources of the river Mersey and had stood, rain-drenched and bewildered, in Mersey Square, Stockport, unable to find any evidence of a river. Too many people from Liverpool think of the Mersey as the wide stretch of water from New Brighton up to the Runcorn Bridge, yet this is just the tidal estuary, the final stretch of the river.

Near the Pier Head the river is less than a mile wide, and the tidal currents here are fierce. This has helped prevent the silting that destroyed the Dee as a navigable river. The narrow stretch of river extends inland for only a couple of miles before widening out to three miles between Speke and Ellesmere Port: a sheet of unbroken water at high tide, but huge stretches of sandbank with narrow channels of water at low. From Seaforth to Garston there is no evidence of the natural shoreline because of the long line of docks and the Otterspool Promenade, but near the village of Hale, with its lighthouse, it is possible to gain some impression of what the shore used to be like. The saltmarsh at Pickerings Pasture near Hale Bank had been used as a rubbish dump in the 1930s, but now there is a

The Runcorn Widnes, or Silver Jubilee, road bridge in the foreground was built in the early 1960s to cross both the Mersey and the Manchester Ship Canal, replacing the 1905 Transporter Bridge. The earlier, 1868, rail bridge can just be glimpsed beyond. Before that date, the lowest bridge across the river had been the medieval one at Warrington.
AUTHOR

A ship passes the Seaforth radar station heading out into the Irish Sea. Plans have been mooted to replace the tower with a tall observatory. The hills of north Wales can be seen on the horizon.

pleasant walk along the river up to the Runcorn Bridge and beyond on what is part of the Trans Pennine Trail. The path crosses a new bridge over the Ditton Brook, a tidal creek off the river which must surely give a reasonably accurate impression of what the upper parts of the old Liver Pool would originally have looked like. There is even some surviving evidence of an old timber wharf which had been used by local industry.

The river between Runcorn and Warrington is relatively easy to see as it zig-zags across its flood plain, in places running alongside the Sankey (St Helens) Canal whose locks lead down to the river near the massive power station at Fiddler's Ferry. The town of Warrington owed its growth to the fact that it was the lowest bridging point on the river until the developments between Widnes and Runcorn centuries later. Upstream from Warrington the river flows through Rixton, Warburton, Hollins Green, Cadishead, Flixton and Urmston.

Even though it has a modest flow of water, as the river approaches Greater Manchester it has exerted a strong influence on roads and urban development. From Urmston eastwards to Stockport, the M60 Manchester Ring Road actually follows the river valley. In one sense the Mersey does not exist beyond Stockport because it is there that the Tame, the Etherow and the Goyt are united and come to be known as the Mersey. I decided that my exploration should take me along the banks of the Goyt towards Marple, New Mills and Whaley Bridge. From that point on we moved through open country, and the road began to rise steeply, following the deep valley of the Goyt in the direction of Buxton. A minor twisting and turning single-track road crosses the valley between the Fernilee and Errwood reservoirs. The sound of the Goyt can be heard all along the road as the small but fast-flowing stream drains through Goyt's Moss before passing under the A537 not far from the famous Cat and Fiddle inn. My journey had taken me from tidal estuary, docks, ocean-going vessels and seagulls in the early morning to fast-flowing peat-coloured water, heather, gorse and sheep of the Peak District before the end of the day.

THE LANDSCAPE OF LIVERPOOL

As I stood with a crowd of people on the waterfront at Seacombe looking across to Liverpool over the darkness of the river waiting to see a firework display, we might all have been forgiven for thinking that Liverpool is flat. The great water-front buildings were ablaze with light and seemed to rise, cliff-like, from the shoreline. The height and density of the city-centre buildings have almost completely obliterated the natural topography of the area. However, cyclists and people carrying heavy shopping bags are keenly aware that Liverpool is far from flat. Many road names are a useful reminder of the land-forms below the buildings: Brownlow Hill, Mount Pleasant, Everton Brow and Valley, Parkhill Road, Woolton Hill Road, Mossley Hill Road, Gateacre Brow, Childwall Valley Road – these are but a fraction of the names that come immediately to mind.

One day when poring over the Ordnance Survey map, I became conscious of how the eye finds it very difficult to follow the faint orange contour lines running through densely built-up areas. With desk-lamp, magnifying glass and thin black felt tip pen I began to draw over the contour lines to emphasise them; dramatically the topography of Liverpool began to emerge. To my delight the 10 metre line traced

Evidence of the sandstone ridges running north to south below Liverpool.
AUTHOR

Steep roads of terraced houses near to the Dingle slope towards what used to be the South Docks.
AUTHOR

just to the south of Pier Head revealed the exact position of the old Pool. Wisely the designers of Sefton Park had used the courses of the old Upper and Lower Brooks which fed the River Jordan to form the ribbon lakes, and Otterspool Park was created in the narrow valley through which the water ran to the Mersey.

The original settlers took these geological features into account when positioning their settlement: a tidal creek as safe harbour for small fishing boats; a low sandstone ridge above the dangers of high tide; a well in the sandstone as a supply of good drinking water.

The town is in fact built upon a series of north–south sandstone ridges. The most westerly of these runs down from Bootle through to the original site of Toxteth Park. Despite the density of much of the housing, the height of the land is made clear by some of the vistas to the south and the west. Some of these views became known nationwide in the television series *Bread* which revealed the life of the Boswell family in its little terraced house on a steep street above the Mersey and with views over to Wirral and the Welsh hills beyond. Further inland the Everton Ridge runs south to Mossley Hill. During the nineteenth century the steep westerly slopes of Everton were covered in densely packed terraced houses built in alarmingly steep streets, which must have been lethal in ice and snow, but these have been replaced by the grass slopes of open parkland which provides spectacular views over the river and the Irish Sea. The two cathedrals are built on

17

An old watercourse has been used to create very attractive ribbon lakes that flow through Sefton Park.
AUTHOR

this same ridge. The most easterly ridge stretches further south than the others and reaches Liverpool's highest point, on the tree-covered ridge above the ancient settlement of Woolton. In many places the underlying sandstone is now exposed, usually through human activity in quarrying, tunnels and dramatic railway cuttings.

As many gardeners will point out, much of Liverpool is built on thick layers of boulder clay deposited at the time of the last Ice Age. The clay cliffs of my childhood, which gave access to the 'cast iron' shore at St Michaels, have long been covered by city refuse and the Otterspool Promenade, but the clay cliffs at Thurstaston on the Dee in the Wirral are almost identical to the Liverpool cliffs I remember from my childhood.

Some of the water courses which over thousands of years have eroded their way through rock and clay have disappeared from the surface completely – usually because of human activity. The Ditton Brook still flows southwards from Childwall to enter the Mersey near Pickerings Pasture, not far from Runcorn Bridge. The River Alt is the main waterway running to the north, joined by a number of tributary streams, some of which are now almost completely hidden in culverts.

The district of Tuebrook takes its name from the Tew Brook which rises near Prescot Road but which it now culverted for most of its course. Bootle Brook, Kirkdale Brook and Beacon Gutter whose short courses ran at right angles into the Mersey have now dried completely because of alterations to the water-table as a result of boring and pumping. The stream which once fed the Liver Pool is still running, albeit in a culvert way below the busy streets of the town centre. A little stream known as the Dingle once ran down Park Road near the Ancient Chapel of Toxteth and joined the Mersey near a rocky outcrop which was called Dingle Point. Dickenson's Dingle ran from the southern end of Lodge Lane through Princes Park, under Ullet Road, Aigburth Road and down through St Michael's before reaching the river. Nineteenth-century landscape designers responsible for the construction of Sefton Park made imaginative use of ancient watercourses, with the result that ribbon lakes were created in the courses of the Upper and Lower Brooks and met to feed the levels of the boating lake. Aigburth Vale takes its name from the valley through which the stream originally flowed to enter the river through the Otters Pool, the whole valley is now known as Otterspool Park. The lake in Calderstones Park was also part of an ancient watercourse that ran to the river at Garston.

Ditton Brook near its entry into the Mersey. Although much smaller than the old Pool of Liverpool, this photograph gives a fairly good idea of what the Liver Pool must have looked like at low tide.

AUTHOR

THREE

Seven streets and a castle'

IN THE EARLY YEARS of his reign, King John was anxious to continue the war in Ireland which had been begun by his father, but his lack of a convenient and dependable port of embarkation for his soldiers was a serious hindrance. Chester was the established port of the North West, but it was firmly controlled by the powerful Earl of Chester. Between 26 and 28 February 1206, King John and his retinue were travelling from Lancaster to Chester. The bridging point on the Mersey was at Warrington, and it is unlikely that the king came in person to survey the Mersey shore, but he was certainly advised that the sheltered tidal creek at 'Liverpul' might be an invaluable asset, and that the triangular peninsula to the north of the Pool might be ideal for development as a new borough.

The parchment signed in Winchester on 28 August 1207 is usually referred to as King John's charter, although the term 'letters patent' is more accurate. The original Latin document is preserved in the city to this day:

John by the Grace of God King of England, Lord of Ireland, Duke of Normandy and Aquitaine, Count of Anjou, to all his loyal subjects who may wish to have burgages in the township of Liverpul, greeting. Know ye that we have granted to all our loyal subjects who shall take burgages in Liverpul that they shall have all the liberties and free customs of the township of Liverpul which any free borough of the sea has in our land. And therefore we command you that in safety and in our peace ye shall come thither to receive and occupy our burgages. And in testimony hereof we transmit to you these letters patent. Witness Simon Pateshill. At Winchester the 28th day of August in the 9th year of our reign.

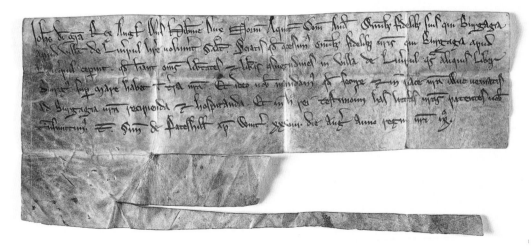

One of the city's most important possessions: King John's 'Charter', signed at Winchester on 28 August 1207. Strictly speaking this was not a charter at all, but letters patent, an early form of open letter inviting people to buy land and to settle in the new, free town of Liverpool that John proposed to build. Henry III gave Liverpool a proper borough charter in 1229.

The earliest remaining record of street names dates from 1300, almost a century after the town was established, but this gives what surely must be an accurate ground-plan of the borough when it was founded, a ground-plan which would remain largely unchanged for four hundred years. The H-shaped grid of the streets is still discernible today and Castle Street, Dale Street and Chapel Street have even retained their original names. It is not known how many people originally lived in the town but by 1296 there are records of 168 families.

King John's 'charter' was important because it marks the beginning of the settlement and because it attracted free men into the new borough. The really significant charter, however, was purchased from King Henry III for £6 13s. 4d. in 1229. It permitted them to elect their own officers instead of the royal bailiff; they no longer had to attend the 'hundred courts' at West Derby; they were freed from the payment of royal tolls, and most important of all they were permitted to establish a Guild which would regulate all trade within the borough. The king still had rights, rents and tolls and fees and fines which were collected on his behalf by a royal bailiff. The astute burgesses made a deal whereby, for an annual payment of £10, they collected all the dues and so freed themselves from the powers of the bailiff. Ramsay Muir has written, 'In this way the burgesses got rid of the royal bailiff; and so long as their lease lasted, they were left as a surprisingly independent, self-governing community, electing their own officers, running their own courts, paying their rents to themselves, working their own mills and ferry, and not meddled with by any outside authority.' The agreement with Henry III did not last for ever and there were occasional reversals of fortune, but Liverpool did achieve four hundred years of relative freedom and stability.

One can walk along the modern equivalents of King John's seven streets without seeing any evidence of the original thirteenth-century buildings. Most of those buildings were, of course, impermanent, probably constructed mainly from wood and clay. The frames of the houses were made of oak beams and the spaces were filled with 'wattle' (light woven timbers), plastered with 'daub' (mud and clay). The houses opened straight on to the narrow, unpaved street and the twenty-first century would have found the whole place filthy. Open areas to the rear must have resembled smallholding rather than our notion of garden. Pigs

The view of Derby Square, the site of the medieval Liverpool Castle, north-north-west along Castle Street towards the eighteenth-century Town Hall.

would be herded out daily to forage on the heath land beyond the Pool, and more than half of the householders made most of their living from farming – the crops being grown on their two strips, about two acres in extent, out in the town fields to the north of the settlement.

The best vantage point was the rocky outcrop in the angle between the Pool and the river. It was some forty feet above sea level and the obvious site for a strong stone castle. The modern Castle Street leads southwards towards Derby Square and the Victoria Monument, the site of Liverpool Castle which was completed by about 1235 by William de Ferrers. No contemporary representations of the castle exist but some painstaking research by E.W. Cox at the end of the nineteenth century gives what is thought to be a fairly reliable account of

The Tower, the Liverpool headquarters of the Stanley family. The Tower was demolished in the nineteenth century, but twentieth-century Tower Building occupies the same site next to the parish church.

The ruined remains of two of the round towers of Flint Castle. Its situation the shores of the Dee is not unlike the site of Liverpool Castle. The curious might also explore an astonishing replica of Liverpool Castle on Rivington Moor.

AUTHOR

the structure. The building was roughly fifty yards square and surrounded by a dry moat twenty yards wide. The turreted curtain wall connected the gatehouse with its bridge and portcullis with three round towers at the other corners. Local sandstone was used and the material for at least one of the towers was quarried in nearby Toxteth Park. The earliest existing written account is from a century later but it recorded, 'four towers, a hall, chamber, chapel, brewhouse and bakehouse with a well therein, a certain orchard and a dovecote.'

The castle was garrisoned only when necessary, but we have some idea of its strengths from the list of equipment, which included 186 pallet beds, 107 spears, 39 lances and fifteen great catapults The Molyneux family, related to the Earls of Sefton, for many years held the office of Constable. Domestically the castle must have been under its greatest stress in 1323 when King Edward II spent a whole week in residence – the longest stay (to date) that any monarch has ever enjoyed in Liverpool.

By 1257 a little stone chapel by the name of St Mary del Key had been built in the town, almost on the shore line and probably just below the tower of the present parish church. A new and larger chapel which was dedicated to St Mary and St Nicholas was built between 1355 and 1361. This was a forerunner of Liverpool Parish Church, known affectionately as St Nick's, although it gained parish status only at the end of the seventeenth century. Before then worshippers had to contend with the three-mile walk out to St Mary's church in Walton which was the parish church until 1699. Originally burials had to take place out at Walton, although when the little township was hit by plague in 1361 the Bishop of Lichfield licensed the churchyard at Our Lady and St Nicholas for burials, and the following year the chapel was consecrated for worship.

Despite the scourge of plague outbreaks, including the Black Death of 1349 which decimated the population, the little borough made progress throughout the fourteenth century. In 1307 the burgesses gained twelve acres of the Moss Lake, the marshy area between modern Hope Street and Crown Street, which provided peat for fuel. By the end of the century they had acquired the rights to the 'waste', the land on the other side of the Pool, although it was many years before buildings spread there. By 1328 there is record of all the streets being paved – a most unusual feature at such an early date.

Currently at the bottom of Water Street and adjacent to the church yard is a large twentieth-century structure called Tower Building. The name is a clue to what used to stand there. In the medieval period there were few stone buildings in the borough but the Stanley family, Earls of Derby, put up a substantial stone structure and in 1406 Sir John Stanley was licensed by King Henry IV to fortify his house with battlements. It survived until 1821 – about a hundred years longer than the castle. The Moore family were influential people in the town but now nothing is left of their house but a street name – Old Hall Street.

Probably the richest and most important family among the burgesses in the fourteenth century was the one which used the name of the town as its name and fortunately there is at least some documentary evidence about William son of Adam Liverpool who became the town's first mayor in 1351. Under his direction at the portmoot court the burgesses tried to regulate the day-to-day affairs and conditions of life. They had to try to ensure that each burgess kept the street in front of his property reasonably clean; the burgesses were responsible for maintaining a night watch to ensure security; and when fire broke out in the tightly clustered timber buildings they had to try to control it.

We know at least something about trade and crafts in the borough shortly before William died because records for 1378 list the activities of the following: 3 weavers, 4 drapers, 2 tailors, 1 bow maker, 1 tanner, 4 boot makers, 5 leather workers, 5 fish merchants, 2 smiths and 18 brewers. There were two Mersey ferries from Wirral, one run by the Prior of Birkenhead and the other by the burgesses themselves. A man on foot was charged a farthing (¼d.), a horseman 2d. and the charges were doubled on market days.

Throughout the medieval period agriculture was the most important local activity, but because of the town charters' favourable terms, trade was becoming increasingly important. Apart from fishing, most of the sea trade was with Ireland, which exported hides and wool through Liverpool and received woollen cloth from Lancashire and Yorkshire in return. Liverpool had its own weekly market on a Saturday which drew traders from both sides of the Mersey and an annual fair on St Martin's Day in November.

In our eyes the changes and developments in Liverpool during the first three centuries of its life seem extremely slow. The township was small and isolated, relying heavily on agriculture and fishing. The streets, though paved, were narrow and dirty. The houses were modest wooden structures without water supply or sanitation, and plague was a constant threat.

THE CASTLE

There is no trace of it today, but for five hundred years Liverpool had a castle. How the Capital of Culture, the World Heritage Site and city tourism chiefs must regret its demolition! Though nineteenth- and twentieth-century archaeology has found evidence for its existence, not a single stone remains visible above ground because in the eighteenth century a church was built on the site and in the early twentieth century the site was crowned with a monstrous statue of Queen Victoria above a block of public toilets. The road running from what is now the Town Hall towards this Victoria Monument, has since the earliest days of the layout of the town been called Castle Street. Just as Chapel Street led to St Mary del Key and later the Church of St Nicholas, so Castle Street led to the Castle.

This nineteenth-century conjectural drawing of Liverpool Castle was based on detailed research carried out by Edward Cox. The gatehouse faced Castle Street. The isolated building near the Pool is the dovecot.
LIVERPOOL RECORD OFFICE

The Victoria Monument occupies part of the site of the original castle.
AUTHOR

Before the construction of the tall buildings of more recent times, the triangular-shaped projection of land, rising to a rocky outcrop 40 feet above river level, protected on one side by the river and the other side by the Pool, would have appeared as the natural site for a castle to defend the new township.

By 1235, within a generation of the foundation of Liverpool, its castle was complete; exactly five hundred years later, 1726, the very last of the ruins had been removed. Throughout this period the castle stood as the largest building in the town, completely dominating even the largest houses of any of the inhabitants. A lengthy paper delivered by Edward W. Cox in 1890 appears to take account of all the surviving evidence from pictures, maps and a wide range of documents. One of the earliest descriptive accounts of the building dates back to 1347, and listed 'four towers, a hall, chamber, chapel, brewhouse and bakehouse, with a well therein, a certain orchard and a dovecot'. Cox had concluded that only two visual representations could be regarded as reliable: a painting held by the Peters family along with an engraving based upon it by John Eyes in 1689; and plans drawn up for Prince Rupert in 1644 by an engineer called Gomme, at the time of the Civil War. Cox's researches indicate that the castle was surrounded by a dry ditch maybe thirty feet wide and up to thirty feet deep. In 1704 Liverpool Corporation said that the whole site measured 6,273 square yards. The only entrance to the castle was from Castle

The imposing eighteenth-century wing of Croxteth Hall, the home of the Molyneux family.
AUTHOR

Street by way of a causeway and bridge through the barbican and between the square towers of the gatehouse. There were eventually three round towers, although one was not part of the original design. The dovecot, an important part of food supply, stood outside the wall on the south side, and the orchard ran down to the Pool on the east.

Cox also pointed out the similarities between Liverpool Castle, now long gone, and Flint Castle, which remains as a substantial ruin on the north Wales coast. The sites of the two castles were also remarkably similar, one on rock foundations on the shore of the Mersey and the other on the Dee. Flint can give us a reasonably clear idea of what Liverpool Castle might have looked like and, to the surprise of many visitors, so can an extraordinary twentieth-century building on the shores of the Lower Rivington reservoir. For there one may find a remarkable reconstruction of Liverpool Castle. The philanthropist the first Lord Leverhulme (of Sunlight Soap fame) had built a large factory and model village for his workers at Port Sunlight on the Wirral. Born in Bolton, he had many connections with the Rivington area, and in later life gave to the public a large area of what is now Rivington Country Park. In 1912 he began to build a full-scale model of Liverpool Castle on the shores of the lake. Leverhulme's builders must have made use of the research and conjecture of Edward Cox and whether or not all details are historically accurate Leverhulme's castle does help us to visualise the original which was such a dominating feature of the Liverpool built environment for five hundred years.

Cox was even able to write from his own experience of an underground passage which ran under what is now James Street, down to the shoreline. This could well have been used to bring supplies from the river or as an escape route from the castle to waiting boats. Castle Moat House, formerly a bank, in Derby Square has deep cellars actually built into what had one been the castle moat.

STANLEY AND MOLYNEUX

Although they did not cross the channel with William the Conqueror in 1066, the Stanley family, taking their name from Stanleigh – stony clearing – near Leek in Staffordshire, is very ancient. The family has many branches across the country, and a recent authoritative genealogical work runs to 541 pages. Members of the family distinguished themselves in battle from early days, but their fortunes rose dramatically on 27 October 1485 when Lord Thomas Stanley was created first Earl of Derby by the first Tudor king, Henry VII, after his victory at Bosworth and the death of Richard III. This is the second oldest earldom in the country. The main family home is at Knowsley, eight miles to the east of Liverpool, and much of the estate is now given over to the animals of the Knowsley Safari Park.

The Molyneux family established their family seat not far away at Croxteth and they became the Earls of Sefton, and Derby and Sefton were to become the most powerful baronial families in south Lancashire. They both had significant strongholds right in the centre of Liverpool: the Molyneux in the Castle and the Stanleys on the shore line in a stone building known for centuries as the Tower – the early twentieth-century Tower Building was constructed on the site of the old Tower, which had been fortified by Sir John Stanley as early as 1406. The Tower became an important embarkation point for the family who from 1403 until 1737 were Kings of the Isle of Man, with Castle Rushen as their ancestral home. There were times when family rivalries were so strong that bloodshed seemed inevitable. In 1424 the Sheriff of Lancaster had to prevent open war between 2,000 supporters led by Thomas Stanley and 1,000 led by Sir Richard Molyneux, ready to do battle on the site of the old Moss Lake. The presence of two such powerful families must at times have been alarming for the burgesses of Liverpool.

The Castle, the Tower and the church of Our Lady and Saint Nicholas were the only substantial stone buildings in the borough. Castle and Tower have both gone but two extensive estates outside the city boundaries remain as reminders of the noble and powerful families. When the last of the Earls of Sefton died in 1972, Croxteth Hall and park were given to the city of Liverpool. The hall itself contains examples of buildings from Elizabethan to Edwardian. The Queen Anne range is the finest section and it is enormously impressive.

There is a mention of Knowsley in the late eleventh-century Domesday survey, and the oldest sections built of stone are thirteenth-century, added to by the first earl in the fifteenth century to accommodate King Henry VI. Extensive additions were made in brick in the eighteenth century and the worst parts of this work were demolished in the 1950s. The 18th Earl 'retained everything which was essential or historically interesting, and while so doing, he reduced the size of the house to a residence more in keeping with the needs of the present day'.

WILLIAM LIVERPOOL

During the medieval period very little is recorded about the lives of individuals. Fortunately, and probably because they were the tenants of the two windmills where all the grain of the borough was ground, we have some information about two ancient families: the Moores and the Liverpools.

The Liverpools might well have lived in the area before the borough was established, and they certainly occupied a prominent position within in the new community. The man whose life is best recorded was William, son of Adam, who lived in the middle of the fourteenth century at a time when fifteen burgages were held by members of the family. He was tenant of Eastham Mill, built on the site of the ancient watermill behind what is now the Walker Art Gallery. He also had a bakery on Castle Street, a fishery somewhere on the Toxteth shore, and he was a farmer. There may have been others before him, but Adam Liverpool was the first recorded mayor in 1351, and he held office eleven times. He was a leading figure in the construction of the new church, Our Lady and Saint Nicholas, near to Saint Mary del Key at the bottom end of Chapel Street, and his body was actually buried within the church itself. His will, drawn up in 1380, is one of the most important documents from the medieval period.

> *Last Will and Testament of William Fitzadam of Liverpool. In the name of God. Amen. I, William the son of Adam, being of sound mind, though weak in body, make my last will in this manner. Imprimis, I bequeath my soul to God, and the Blessed Virgin Mary and all the Saints; and my body to be buried in the chapel of Liverpool, before the face of the white image of the Virgin, which is my perpetual place of burial. I leave to be distributed in bread on the day of my burial, three quarters of wheat. I leave six pounds of wax to be used about my body. I leave to every priest in the chapel of Liverpool 4 pence. I leave the rest of all my goods to Katherine my wife and our children. To perform my will I appoint as my executors, John le Fuller, and William Parker, chaplain. Given at Liverpool on the Tuesday next before the feast of St Luke the Evangelist, in the presence of Thomas de la More, the Mayor, and John de Eccleston, and others of my neighbours, in the year 1380.*

He was Liverpool's richest man and at his death the bulk of his wealth lay in animals and farm produce. Grain in his barn was worth £6 13s. 4d.; growing strips of wheat £7; nine cows and oxen were worth 10s. each; six horses 7s. and eighteen pigs 1s. 6d. The total value of household furniture and utensils amounted only to £7 6s. 8d.

The other town mill, Townsend Mill, was on the site of what is now the Wellington Column and was held by the Moore family, significant leaders in the community over several centuries. They held a lot of land both in the borough and in the surrounding villages. Their main house called Moore Hall was on the northern edge of the borough and the croft ran down to the river. They bought land in Kirkdale and built a new country house called Bank Hall. Their Old Hall is remembered now only in a street name.

OUR LADY AND SAINT NICHOLAS

The people of Liverpool have worshipped on a site at the south-west corner of Chapel Street since 1257. From the very earliest days of the borough there was a small stone-built chapel of Saint Mary del Key which stood near to what is now the north-west corner of what is affectionately known to everyone as Saint Nick's, Liverpool parish church. Unfortunately all evidence of the earliest building has disappeared.

For centuries it was one of the most prominent buildings on the waterfront, but now the church of Our Lady and Saint Nicholas is increasingly dwarfed by surrounding buildings. The present tower was completed in 1815, but the main body of the church was badly damaged by a bomb in December 1940.

AUTHOR

33

Walton was the parish church for the whole district, but the township of Liverpool had increased so much in population by the fourteenth century that the construction of a chapel and burial ground in the town seemed sensible and certainly more convenient. During a serious outbreak of plague, the Bishop of Lichfield and Coventry licensed the burial ground so that infected corpses did not have to be carried to Walton, and in 1362 Our Lady and Saint Nicholas was consecrated.

There are no contemporary pictures of the newly built church, and a much later oil painting by an unnamed Dutch artist from around the middle of the seventeenth century is all we have to go on. The later engraving of the whole townscape by John Eyes presents us with the clearest impression of what the ancient church must have looked like and, after the castle, it was clearly the most significant building in the early town. Since the expansion of the dock system, at George's

The church after the reordering of the interior after the war. The sanctuary is now at the west end under the tower.
AUTHOR

Dock and Basin in particular, the parish church has been marooned from the river, but originally it stood right on the riverbank.

Like most ancient churches, St Nick's was added to and modified over the years. By the end of the fifteenth century there was a north aisle. Between 1673 and 1718 the structure underwent a number of modifications and extensions to accommodate the increasing population. In 1699 the church was finally elevated to become a parish church. Galleries were built in a rather unsystematic manner. The parish books for 11 September 1745 recorded details of a significant extension: 'It is ordered by this vestry that a spire shall be built on the tower of the parochial chapel of St Nicholas, and that a plan thereof be in the meantime drawn by Mr. Thomas See, and that proposals for the building of it be delivered to the present church wardens, Messrs. Hugh Ball and Samuel Seel, who are to lay them before the next meeting of the vestry.' What the congregation decided to do at St Nick's was extraordinary: they retained the interior galleries and rented pews and rebuilt the walls around the existing interior.

The tower housed a peal of bells which were rung regularly, but some people were becoming concerned about the structural stability of the tower, given that its new spire was supported by the original foundations. On the morning of Sunday 11 February 1810, as the people were assembling for worship, spire and tower collapsed and crashed through the roof of the church just as a group of girls were entering from the Moorfields Charity School. Three adults and twenty-three girls were killed instantly and a further child died later in hospital.

Thomas Harrison, architect from Chester, was commissioned to design a new tower; with its highly distinctive open stone lantern, this was built between 1811 and 1815. It is this tower that remains today as such a distinctive feature of the Pier Head. The tower is unchanged, but the main part of the church is not. On 21 December 1940 the building was hit by a German incendiary bomb and the interior was completely gutted, although the tower survived. By means of the construction of a small, temporary wooden building within the burnt-out shell, worship on the site continued. In March 1949, rebuilding began to the design of Edward Butler and the new building was dedicated for worship on St Luke's Day 1952.

Medieval worshippers would not recognise the building: it was completely re-orientated, with the altar adjacent to the tower at the west end. Two charred timbers from the original building form a cross behind the altar in the St Peter's Chapel. The great suspended rood over the sanctuary depicts the crucified Christ with Mary and John, and this was carved from timber from the old bell frame. In the Maritime Chapel there is a figure of St Mary del Key made by Liverpool sculptor, Arthur Dooley.

During the early centuries, all of the worshippers lived close to their church; nowadays very few people actually live in the parish, although the church continues to minister on a daily basis to the local commercial community. Recently there has actually been a discernible move back towards city living and a consequent increase in the population of the parish.

The Old School House in Woolton, early seventeenth century, is still used for educational purposes.

**MUCH WOOLTON
OLD SCHOOL
DAY NURSERY**
WOOLTON   428 1101

FOUR

'An insignificant and decaying borough'

T H E Liverpool of 300 years ago would be completely unrecognisable to us. The shoreline from Seaforth to Garston was quite undeveloped, and not a single building of the town of that time is still in existence today. To us, used to the rapid growth of Liverpool in the nineteenth and twentieth centuries, the first three centuries of the town's history look quiet, sluggish, even stagnant.

The fifteenth century was an uneasy age for the fortunes of Liverpool. There were frequent negotiations over the charter and the farm-fee lease, and eventually the burgesses could not even raise enough money to pay the annual rent. The great local families – Molyneux in the Castle and Stanley in the Tower – must have been intimidating to the burgesses and the Wars of the Roses caused unease and disturbance throughout Lancashire, though there were no reports of hostilities within Liverpool itself.

Instead of showing steady growth, the population declined. In 1346 the population has been estimated at about 1,200 but by 1565 it had dropped to about 700. The Black Death in Liverpool in 1361 has already been noted, but plague outbreaks continued. As late as 1558 about one-third of the population died; the annual fair was cancelled and the weekly market was suspended for three months. However, despite outbreaks of disease, the sixteenth century gave evidence that the fortunes of Liverpool would rise again. Like John before him, king Henry VIII needed Liverpool and Chester to transport troops to Ireland and provide provisions.

Part of Stanlawe Grange, the oldest building in Liverpool. The very earliest part dates from 1291, but much of the early fabric has been lost, and the building has been converted into two houses.
AUTHOR

There were some significant developments at this time. The generosity of John Crosse in 1515 led to the establishment of a grammar school, possibly in the old St Mary del Key building, and he presented a 'new house called Our Lady's House, to keep their courts and such business as they shall think most expedient'. Through this generous act Liverpool acquired its first town hall, on High Street. Meanwhile, in 1580 there was a substantial change to the local government of the borough which had, to that date, been in the hands of the Assembly of the Burgages. Lord Mayor Edward Halsall proposed a new system whereby a council of twenty-four members and twelve aldermen would be given authority to govern the borough. This self-elected town council held control of the town for some 250 years, until the Municipal Reform Act of 1835.

'Insignificant and decaying' the borough may have been, but from 1550 onwards we do at least know far more about Liverpool because of the mass of material recorded in the Liverpool Town Books which span the period from 1550 to 1835. 'Insignificant' it might have been, but many of the trading details in the records from the middle of the sixteenth century indicate that the freemen of Liverpool had established some very astute deals which were to lead the borough from its principally agricultural past towards a far more profitable, trading future. For one three-month period in 1586 we have a detailed record of vessels trading in and out of Liverpool. Sixteen vessels arrived from Ireland carrying linen yarn, much of this sent on for finishing to Manchester, and also hides, sheepskins and tallow. No fewer than seventeen ships sailed from the port carrying coal from the Wigan mines, linen cloth from Manchester and Kendal, and woollen cloth from Yorkshire. Smaller items included knives and scythes from the metal workers of Sheffield, leather goods and a variety of 'smallwares'. There were also two or three merchants trading with Spain and Portugal at this time, importing mainly good quality iron and wine.

It is the manner in which trading was tightly regulated by the borough for the good of itself and its freemen that is most intriguing for the modern mind.

Before a ship could even anchor, it was boarded by a water-bailiff. If the owner was not a freeman, he had to pay anchorage and wharfage money. The cargo could not then simply be sold. The mayor had to negotiate the terms on which the cargo could be traded. The first way was to make what was called a 'town's bargain' for which the price was fixed by the merchant 'prysors', who valued the cargo, oversaw the unloading and weighing and collected the 'weighage dues'. All the goods were carried up to the town warehouse below the arches of the town hall and there the merchants were charged 'hallage dues'. After this the freemen were entitled to buy a share of the cargo at the set price.

If the ship owner did not like the 'town's bargain' price he was offered, he could try to negotiate the sum he would have to pay for a licence to try to sell the goods at his own price. That was not the end of regulation and profit for the freemen. The importers were allowed to sell only to the freemen, who might make their own profit by selling on to others. After this there were strict regulations about selling on market day: 'no townsfolk, neither men, women nor servants shall buy any butter, eggs or fish before the same are brought to the usual place of market', and there were limits to the quantity of grain a trader might buy on one day.

There were strict procedures to be adhered to at the Saturday market – right down to where people had to stand. The traders from Lancashire had to line up their own sacks on the east side of Castle Street and the Cheshire men on the west. The mayor then made his inspection, attended by the 'levelookers', to check the accuracy of the measures which were being used. For the first hour only the freemen were allowed to buy.

All of these regulations must have been very hard on those who were selling but certainly lined the pockets of the freemen of Liverpool. It was no longer necessary to inherit a burgage to become a freeman. People were 'elected' to the status but only after the payment of the appropriate fee. Sons of freemen were charged 3s. 4d. and apprentices double that sum. On top of this, some rents were received from patches of land over on 'the waste', the land over on the other side of the Pool.

Strict regulation was not confined to the market or matters of trade. The church was also under the control of the officers of the borough, who were responsible for the upkeep of the fabric and for the appointment of the parson, whose tenure of office was most uncertain as he was appointed, 'during the time he useth himself well and in good sort, but yet always to be removed at the appointment of the mayor and his brethren.' Their complaints were many and various. One parson was fined 'for suffering the churchyard to be spoiled with swine'; another was forced to pay 6d. for cutting down a tree and 'for keeping horses and kine in the churchyard'. Another poor incumbent was told 'to cut his hair to a comely and seemly length, as best beseemeth a man in his place'. All that for only £10 a year and a house! The poor sexton fared even worse, with wide-ranging tasks including being required to 'sing his plain-song and prick-song and play on the organs', keep the dogs out of the church, ring the curfew bell for half an hour from 7 p.m. from October to February, and ensure the accuracy of the clock, 'The clerk shall have no wages unless he look well to the keeping of the clock.'

In view of all that was to happen later, it is ironic that Liverpool prospered considerably through Elizabeth I's military expeditions to devastate Ireland. Large numbers of troops passed through the town and were allowed 3d. for every meal eaten during what was sometimes a long wait for transport and good weather. The ship owners earned at least £1 for each man transported. The mayor and his burgesses had to keep order and quell any violent disturbances which broke out among the troops. One Sunday morning in 1573 the mayor had to call out his company to parade on the waste over the Pool, 'every man with his best weapons' and 'as eager as lions'. The show of strength had the desired effect in controlling a certain Captain Bartley. There was a strong sense of corporate responsibility that the town be maintained in good order. A terrible storm in 1561 had smashed the harbour wall, so 'the mayor called the whole town together unto the hall, where they counselled all in one consent for the foundation and making of a new haven.' 'On the Monday morning then next, the mayor, and of every house in Water street one labourer, went to the old Pool and there began and enterprised digging, ditching and busily labouring upon the foundation of the new haven; and so the Tuesday, of every house in the Castle Street.'

Bull-baiting and cock-fighting were popular entertainments, and the mayor supported an annual four-mile horse race on Kirkdale Sands. But the spirit of government in the town was becoming more puritanical and there was a firm hand to control 'the exceeding number of alehouses and tippling-houses'. Bowling allies and gambling were suppressed; apprentices who were caught playing cards were whipped and 'no manner of apprentice or servant shall depart out of their

Liverpool has very few ancient buildings; indeed within the old boundaries Bluecoat Chambers is the oldest. The few buildings to survive in what are now the suburbs therefore take on great significance. This is the Old School House (early seventeenth-century) in the shadow of the church of Saint Mary at Walton.
AUTHOR

master's or dame's house after eight of the clock, unless it be on his master or dame's business, on pain of imprisonment.' Whoever they might be, bachelors were not allowed on the streets after nine o'clock. In 1592 even the mayor was fined because his house guest did not go to church on the Sabbath.

By the end of the Tudor period, the little borough was holding its own, maybe just beginning to thrive, but the township at the end of Elizabeth's reign still strongly resembled the new town that King John had established in 1207.

The little settlements adjacent to Liverpool must be remembered. During the Middle Ages the burgesses had been zealous in maintaining the boundaries of their borough, which they walked and inspected annually. By the middle of the sixteenth century there are reports of the formal walking of the boundaries every seven years on Easter Monday. On the landward side, Liverpool was encircled by a number of ancient settlements, older than itself, though destined centuries later largely to lose their identity and become mere districts of Liverpool.

Kirkdale is now thought of as a rather ill-defined district associated with the north docks, Scotland Road and the way through to Walton. It lay immediately to the north of the old borough and was always associated with the Moore family: their original Old Hall was within the boundaries near what is now Old Hall Street. They built their new house, Bank Hall, on a site near present day Sandhills Station. Chirchedele was recorded in the Domesday Book, but by the nineteenth century Kirkdale and its docks and densely populated little streets was incorporated into Liverpool.

The Liverpool boundary did not extend as far as Walton, but for centuries, the people of Liverpool had to travel through Kirkdale to the parish church in Walton. It has been estimated that there has been a church on the site of Walton church for at least a thousand years and it still retains a Saxon font. The original wooden building was replaced by a stone church in 1361, while its nineteenth-century replacement was largely destroyed by bomb damage. The oldest building now is the stone-built, seventeenth-century school.

The ancient settlement of Everton lay inland from Kirkdale and occupied one of the most prominent positions of any of the ancient settlements, right on top of the sandstone ridge. This ridge rises to 250 feet at the highest point and has always been one of the most prominent geographical features in the region. It offers superb views and is usually fresh and breezy. Sir James Picton has recorded that the population of Everton in 1327 was little more than 100; in 1790 it was still only 370 but by 1816 the population must have been just over 1,000, as more and more people moved away from the grime of the town centre to take up residence on Everton's slopes. On the site of the present St George's church, and probably dating back to the reign of Elizabeth I, there was a sandstone beacon about 18 feet square and between 25 and 30 feet in height. A little turret projected upwards at one corner to house the beacon fire.

The largest and most significant neighbouring district was West Derby. Historically it was one of the six hundreds (districts) of Lancashire, the place where the lord of the hundred held his court. The Saxons built a wooden fort and the Normans replaced this with a small motte and bailey castle at the heart of a sizeable forest stretching for 11 miles from Thornton near Crosby to Blackbrook near St Helens. King John's Liverpool 'Charter' put the nail into the West Derby coffin as far as its power and significance in the region was concerned. For centuries it remained essentially rural in character. It is interesting to note that the two great and powerful families of Liverpool, the Molyneux and the Stanleys established great country houses and estates near to each other here as well, at Croxteth and Knowsley. A stone cottage from about 1600 and the courthouse from 1662 are the oldest existing buildings.

Toxteth is the last neighbouring district whose bounds were walked, and this area, though not part of Liverpool until the nineteenth century, has long associations with the borough because it was acquired as a royal hunting park by King John in the thirteenth century. Stochestede, a stockaded area, was mentioned in Domesday as was Esmedune, smooth down, modern Smithdown. It was established with a master huntsman, forty-nine men, ten horses, two packs of dogs and fifty-two spaniels, and the whole area was fenced. Despite all the careful tending, neither King John nor any other English monarch has ever hunted there. In modern terms, the area is clearly defined as extending from a gateway on Parliament Street where St James's church now stands to Otterspool, and from the line of Smithdown Road right down to the shores of the Mersey. As a child, I could never understand why the term Toxteth Park was still in current use because so much of the area was completely covered with dense-packed houses, but even then it was possible from the top deck of a tram on the higher ground in Mill Street to catch exciting steep views down to the river and the Clwyd Hills beyond and down towards the rocky outcrops at Frodsham and Helsby on the Cheshire plain.

In its early days Toxteth must have been one of the most attractive districts adjacent to Liverpool. The shoreline, particularly where a steam flowed into the river at the Dingle and the Oskelbrook broadened out in what is now Otterspool Park, must have been especially picturesque. The name Lodge Lane on the eastern side of Sefton Park gives a hint to the fact that it led to an ancient hunting lodge. A second lodge was much nearer to the river and was finally demolished because of the building of the railway and Otterspool Station. The area remained as woodland until the seventeenth century.

SPEKE HALL

Speke was not to become part of Liverpool until well into the twentieth century, but because really old buildings in the region are so rare, Speke Hall becomes even more significant, although Stanlawe Grange in modern Aigburth Hall Avenue is considered to be the oldest building in Liverpool, possibly dating back as far as 1291.

In 2003 in *England's Thousand Best Houses*, Simon Jenkins awarded Speke five stars, placing it among his top twenty houses in the country, in the company of such famous places as Chatsworth, Hampton Court, Blenheim and the Royal Pavilion in Brighton. Speke Hall was home to the Norris family and was largely complete by 1598. Though in terms of furniture, decoration and use there have been many changes, the basic structure of the house remains as it was built.

The finished building was a big house, home to a rich and landed Lancashire family. Most of the population inhabited something far less grand, but the principles of the structure of a half-timbered house remain the same. All four wings at Speke rest upon a base of red local sandstone. All the oak timbers were carefully cut and marked on the ground before the erection process began; mortice and tenon joints were secured by oak pegs. The basic frame is filled in with wattle and daub: slivers of oak and hazel twigs are interwoven and daubed with a mixture of clay, cow dung and chopped straw finished with a layer of lime plaster. Most of the elaborate timberwork on the outside of the walls is purely decorative and was certainly never painted black before the nineteenth century. The timber roof frame is clad in sandstone slabs.

The eighteenth century was a bad time for the hall, when it was neglected and mistreated, but its restoration lay with members of the Watt family. The first Richard Watt was a Liverpool merchant. The fifth Richard Watt inherited the house in 1855 and lived in it as his family home. He refurnished the hall and laid out the surrounding gardens and land. The house and estate are now well cared for by the National Trust, and the whole area is like an historical oasis, close to the industrial and housing areas of Speke and almost underneath the flight path of the Liverpool John Lennon Airport. To tour through the house, to stand beneath the ancient yew trees in the central courtyard and to walk quietly through the gardens and near to the river is a wonderful experience, one that I remember well from a school trip to Speke many decades ago.

The Cavalier Prince Rupert surveyed the little township of Liverpool from the top of Everton ridge, a site that still provides panoramic views across the city and out to sea.

FIVE

'A mere crow's nest' ... ?

F R O M the height of Victorian prosperity in Liverpool in 1873, Sir James Picton commented on the state of the town at the start of the seventeenth century:

> At the commencement of this century, four hundred years had elapsed from the foundation of the borough. Although there had been occasional scintillations of prosperity, yet on the whole the port of Liverpool could not be pronounced a success. The population continued few, and the trade very limited.

Perhaps a rather harsh, Sir James: growth had been impeded, but there were positive signs that years of stagnation were coming to an end and that the seventeenth century might well be seen as an important turning point in the fortunes of the little community on the Mersey shoreline.

The rise of the Mersey and of Liverpool must be seen alongside the decline in prominence of the Dee and of Chester. In legal terms Chester was still the main port of the North West, the centre of customs; and the mayor of Chester acted as the chief officer for the crown over the transportation of soldiers to Ireland.

The gradual shifting of sandbanks and the inevitable silting of the wide-mouthed estuary of the Dee meant that no large craft could sail anywhere near the old city walls. By 1625, when the city of Chester had no ships, Liverpool had long been a tidal creek and a 'member of the port of Chester'. As early as 1445, Chester's councillors petitioned central government about the silting and sand banks which had

taken away ... the great flow of water ... by which our said merchants had a
course and return ... to our said city ... so that no merchant ship can
approach within twelve miles or more ... to the great detriment, desolation,
and impoverishment of our said city and citizens.

Even in the fourteenth century, larger vessels had to unload heavy cargoes at
Heswall, Neston or Shotwick. By the following century the problem was even
worse leading to the economically disastrous strategy whereby vessels anchored
in the Hyle Lake off the coast at Hoylake. There was no harbour there and all
the goods had to be unloaded by rowing boat and transported by bad roads
down the Wirral to Chester. When soldiers were to be transported to Ireland,
they had to board ship off Hilbre Island. Even the building of the New Haven
at Neston could not save the day. The taxes to be paid on imported goods were
lower in Liverpool than they were in Chester, and so the future of such landing
places as Dawpool at Thurstaston and Redbank at Caldy were numbered and
they could not compete with Liverpool once transatlantic trade with the West
Indies began in the 1660s. By 1618 Liverpool registered twenty-four ships,
amounting to 462 tons. and by mid-century the population had reached
2,000.

The town officials had clung proudly and with determination to their royal
charters right back to King John's time, but in 1626 they were pleased with a
new charter from King Charles I that further consolidated their power, giving
them full rights over the Waste, across the Pool from the main settlement, and
ensured their powers of local government:

Liverpool hereafter shall be a free town of itself, and the burgesses of the same
town and their successors for ever hereafter shall be, by virtue of these presents,
one body corporate and politic in deed and in name, by the name of the
mayor, bailiffs, and burgesses in the town of Liverpool in the county of
Lancaster.

The words were clear but the King was desperately short of money, unable to
pay a debt he had incurred with the city of London, gave the lordship of
Liverpool and various other manors to the city of London in 1628 which, five
years later, they sold on to Sir Richard Molyneux, Constable of the Castle of
Liverpool, no friend of the burgesses.

Apart from the loss of the little chantry chapels and their attendant priests
from Saint Nicholas Church the people of Liverpool were mainly untroubled at
the time of the upheavals of the English Reformation, but during the reign of
Elizabeth the puritans were to become a powerful force in the town. Unsatisfied
with one parson at the church, the burgesses appointed a preacher to be paid

£30 a year and 'a good milk cow'. By 1635 twice a month there were two week-day sermons delivered by visiting puritan clergy. Even before the outbreak of the Civil War, there was a clear split between the puritan burgesses with their parliamentary leanings and most of the great land-owning families of south Lancashire, many of whom were Roman Catholic in sympathy and practice. The Moore family, probably the richest among the burgesses, were staunchly for puritanism and parliament. John became an MP for Liverpool and later was one of the judges who condemned Charles I to be executed.

A significant puritan presence was to be established immediately adjacent to the town when in 1604 Sir Richard Molyneux cleared trees from parts of Toxteth and established twenty small tenant farms worked by families brought from the Bolton area. It is thought that the devout, religious character of the new inhabitants led to some interesting local names: the Holy Land, the River Jordan and Jericho Farm.

The Ancient Chapel of Toxteth was established at the Dingle, although most of the present-day building is of eighteenth-century origin. We know that one Jeremiah Horrocks was born in 1618 in a farmhouse in Otterspool, and that he might have been taught by Richard Mather at the Ancient Chapel. Horrocks was one of Liverpool's greatest sons, relatively little known by local people, but whose contribution to astronomy was hailed by later giants in the field such as Newton and Herschel.

Not long after Horrocks' premature death in 1641, civil war came to Liverpool.

Citizens of Liverpool in the twenty-first century might feel that they know all about civil war, hand-to-hand fighting, heavy artillery on public buildings, rumour, heroism, carnage and unburied corpses. Not in reality of course, but in the more sanitised virtual reality of the television screen and the six o'clock news. Atrocities are committed in Bosnia, Baghhad, Beirut, even Belfast, but all this we see through the edited and organised lens of the BBC cameraman. To be there in the middle of the fighting, house half blown to bits, cut off from family, wounded, without any understanding of exactly what is happening must be truly terrifying. This is exactly what happened to the towns-people of Liverpool during the English Civil War.

Even before the conflict flared, the more knowledgeable of the inhabitants must have feared the worst because, although most of the ordinary towns-folk favoured Parliament, all the great landed families of west Lancashire were staunchly royalist. The Castle and the Tower were under the control of Molyneux and Stanley, and the port, with its strong links with Ireland, was the only signifi- cant port in the whole of the North West. As Roy Strong was to write in *The*

The Ancient Chapel of Toxteth was established at the bottom of Park Road, near the Dingle, in 1618 although it was restored and modified in 1774.

Story of Britain, 'This was to be a very different war from the Wars of the Roses which only affected a few people and a small part of the country. The Civil War was to be a bloody one of skirmishes, battles and sieges affecting virtually the whole country. It was a modern war, fought with firearms whose acrid smoke almost blinded the soldiers.'

In west Lancashire the dominant royalist leader was a Stanley: Lord Strange until he succeeded his father to become Lord Derby in 1643. John Moore was a staunch parliamentarian and a deputy lieutenant. Strange took Preston,

Lancaster and Warrington and in June 1642 he garrisoned Liverpool Castle and captured a store of gunpowder. Colonel Norris of Speke Hall was made governor of the town and built up the stores in the Castle. It is probable that he did not do much to strengthen any of the town's fortifications apart possibly from some work on earth ramparts from Old Hall Street to the bottom of Dale Street. Stanley had repeatedly to send his own forces south leaving him in a very weakened state. He himself had to sail to the Isle of Man leaving his wife in control of a garrison at Lathom House. Colonel Tyldesley was forced to retreat to try to consolidate forces in Liverpool. Unfortunately for him, a parliamentarian warship was in the Mersey, and Colonel Ashton attacked the town with foot soldiers. After two days of fighting, they had captured the houses on the north side of Dale Street and even went so far as to put guns on the tower of Saint Nicholas. There was further fighting in Castle Street and the orchard and fields on the south side of the Castle, the royalists were defeated, with eighty dead and three hundred captured.

The loss of Liverpool was disastrous to the royalist cause because it gave the parliamentarians their only port on the west coast and a good base from which to defeat the final remnants of opposition at Lathom House. The burgesses petitioned to have one of their own number appointed as governor, and in 1644 Colonel John Moore was named. At almost the same time he was appointed vice-admiral. Whether or not all this power in the hands of one man would be good for war-scarred Liverpool, the burgesses had to wait to see.

When the royalist forces had held the town they had done little to establish much in the way of fortifications to the north and they relied upon the Pool to keep them safe from the south. In an attempt to establish a powerful line of defence a German engineer was brought in. He oversaw the digging of a ditch thirty six feet wide and nine feet deep backed by an earth bank formed from the excavations. These fortifications ran from the shore just north of the Old Hall, round Tithebarn Street and then to the Pool. Gates and cannon protected the entrance to Old Hall, Tithebarn and Dale Streets. Cannons were positioned along the line of the Pool itself and on the walls of the castle.

Professional soldiers were drafted in – a regiment of foot soldiers and a troop of cavalry – and they were supplemented by the compulsory military duties of every one of the burgesses, who were fined one shilling if they failed to muster 'at the beating of the drum'. Delay in payment was to be punished with imprisonment. There are reports that the soldiers garrisoned in the town behaved well, but the provision of adequate supplies of food must have proved very difficult. A strict control was enforced upon all the inhabitants, some of whom were expelled from the town:

... it is therefore ordered by the new mayor, the Governor, and the rest of the Common Council of the same town, that all such papists and malignants, except such as are prisoners; as also their wives, children and families, shall within 14 days after notice hereof, depart and remove out of the said town, upon pain to be plundered and deprived of all their goods and personal estate whatsoever.

Strangers and other lodgers and such as are not faithful and trusty to the service of the King and Parliament may be discharged and removed from the town with all speed possible in respect of the present dangers.

Very strict Sunday observance laws were enforced: 'It is ordered that all such house-holders or other persons as shall neglect the strict observance of Sundays and fast days, and shall not frequent the church, but either loiter or stay abroad drinking; or shall be disorderly, and taken in any misconduct, shall be severely punished, and shall forfeit for every offence 40 shillings.'

In the spring of 1644, conditions out at Lathom House had become very difficult. The royalist defence under the Countess of Derby faced hostile forces from Bolton in the east and from Liverpool to the west. To the great personal relief of Lord Derby, in May 1644 Prince Rupert with an army of 10,000 royalists marched north. Bolton was speedily overrun and the Countess was relieved before Rupert and his forces headed towards Liverpool. When he stopped on the ridge above the town on 7 June, Rupert was reported to have remarked disparagingly, 'A mere crow's nest that a parcel of boys might take.' Despite modern tall buildings, the view of 'old Liverpool' from the heights of Everton is dramatic, and may have made Rupert over-confident but an initial attack was repulsed. Trenches were dug along what we know as Lime Street, and guns put into position and for days the town and its castle were bombarded. Fighting continued and Rupert used up 100 barrels of precious gunpowder and lost 1,500 men. Sir John Moore in the castle was not confident of success.

Eventually local knowledge was used to win the day – or rather the night – for during the night of 12 June Caryl Molyneux led a troop under cover of darkness through the fields to the north of the fortifications and made their way through into the town near to the Old Hall and met with no resistance. Many of the townspeople were mistrustful of Governor John Moore, and their unease was justified. Knowing that defeat was inevitable, he took to the river and left the town to its fate: 'he betook himself to the sea, and left the town to the merciless mercy of their enemies, who murdered unhumanly and plundered thievishly.' Despite Moore's departure, street fighting continued and the royalist forces were ruthless and killed 'almost all they met with, to the number of 360, and among others ... some that never bore arms in their lives, yea, one poor blind man.' What was left of any value was plundered: 'whatsoever was desirable was the soldiers' right for their hard service.' The royalists were now in possession of what was left of battle-scarred Liverpool. The triumphant Prince Rupert headed north to relieve York but met defeat there at the battle of Marston Moor.

Parliamentarian forces were determined to reclaim Liverpool, and the third siege of the town began, according to Picton, on 20 August. Lord Derby attacked the besiegers, but his forces were routed and shortly after Colonel Moore sailed back into the Mersey. The weakened forces in the Castle surrendered on 4 November and remained under parliamentary control for the rest of the war. The townspeople might not have been altogether happy with the strong military presence that remained in the town, but they had an indomitable spirit and were determined to negotiate some compensation for their heavy losses. Direct appeal was made to Parliament, which was positive in its response. £20 was granted to help and support those widowed and orphaned by the conflict and 500 tons of timber were awarded – cut from the woods of the main local royalist families – to help restore the buildings. Picot commented in the nineteenth century that the lack of reference to stone and brick indicated that timber-framed houses still remained the norm even though good local stone and clay for bricks were close at hand. Well-built half-timbered houses such as Speke Hall and parts of Rufford Old Hall have survived the centuries, although nothing remains within old Liverpool itself.

Tuebrook House (1615) in West Derby Road is now completely surrounded by nineteenth- and twentieth-century buildings.
AUTHOR

CHESTER AND THE DEE

During the Roman period when Liverpool was nothing at all, Chester was a vitally important settlement, along with York and Caerleon it was a permanent legionary fortress. The present city walls are of medieval origin, but their foundations are Roman, and archaeology has revealed ample and well-preserved evidence of Roman occupation. Very different from the eventual little settlement on the Mersey shore, Chester's communication with the rest of the country was supported by excellent Roman roads.

Centuries later, Chester was far and away the largest and most significant port in the North West. Chester lay on the most direct route between London and Ireland, and it was used constantly during the medieval period to ship troops and military supplies to Dublin in small vessels. From the fourteenth century onwards, the town began to handle wine from France and Spain and high-quality Spanish iron in ships of 80 tons. In administrative terms the port of Chester stretched from Barmouth to Solway, and legally Liverpool was no more than a 'creek' of Chester; the Chester officials collected all the customs dues. Though the fortunes of the port showed many fluctuations, trade increased until the middle of the seventeenth century.

By the fifteenth century, however, the Dee began to silt up. Unlike the Mersey it has a very wide mouth which cannot be scoured out by the tide, while sandbanks in Liverpool Bay and in the estuary itself seriously restricted the flow of water. For a hundred years, larger vessels had not been able to reach Chester itself and Heswall, Neston and Shotwick became the limits of navigation for all the larger sea-going vessels and by the fifteenth century even Redbank at Caldy could not

The original Hyle Lake where passengers and goods were brought ashore by rowing boat. Hilbre Island at the mouth of the River Dee can be seen on the horizon. The island can be reached on foot at low tide.
AUTHOR

save Chester as a port. When the larger ships could no longer enter the estuary safely, they dropped anchor in the Hyle Lake, making it necessary for men and cargo to be brought ashore by rowing boat. From there on, everything had to be transported by cart or pack-horse along inadequate roads down the Wirral peninsula to Chester itself. Altough twenty-first-century Chester is a thriving shopping and tourist centre, it is hard to believe that it was ever a port of any significance. With goods being unloaded at various places down river, it became impossible for customs officials to collect the import dues.

Chester's misfortunes became Liverpool's opportunity. The Liverpool customs dues were lower, and the Pool offered better anchorage than Chester could provide. The result was inevitable: the port of Chester faded completely and the port of Liverpool eventually achieved extraordinarily high levels of growth. One sad result has been the inevitable destruction of the natural shoreline of the Mersey, but the survival of a more unspoiled Dee shore. Where Liverpool developed nine miles of docks, West Kirby built a marine lake. Liverpool dumped its refuse at Otterspool and built a riverside promenade; the river at Parkgate retreated further and further, leaving it as a kind of riverside ghost town with distant memories of Lord Nelson and Lady Hamilton. Building along the shoreline from West Kirby towards Chester has been carefully controlled so that it remains one of the most attractive parts of the Wirral. Liverpool seems far away, but the tower of Liverpool Cathedral is clearly visible from the top of the sandstone ridges at Caldy and Thurstaston, and many people who reside in the attractive villages drive into Liverpool every day to work. Much of the Mersey shore of the Wirral has been spoiled, but many parts of the Dee shore are a delight.

Chester is considerably more ancient than Liverpool. This weir on the river Dee at Chester was originally built more than a century before Liverpool was founded. It held water that was used to power water-mills. Part of the old city wall, built on Roman foundations, is visible on the left.

AUTHOR

JEREMIAH HORROCKS

On a grey, blustery day in February, writer's block led me to abandon my laptop, don a scruffy anorak and go for a walk. Within six minutes I was standing at the bottom of Park Road on the pavement outside the Ancient Chapel of Toxteth. Nothing around me gave a clue to the appearance of that part of the Dingle at the time of Jeremiah Horrocks. The little stream running down Park Road had long gone and the little squat sandstone church is hemmed in by nineteenth- and twentieth-century building – I remember that in my childhood it stood in the shadow of Dingle tram sheds.

The first church was built in 1618, 'restored and modified' in 1774, but the building did make Horrocks a little more real to me. And although there is no trace of the house in which Horrocks was born, I can see the same daily flow of tides; the shoreline might have changed, but the distant view of Wirral remains, as does Moel Fammau and other hills in the Clwydian range. More important is the sky, charted by Horrocks, clear and unchanging (despite modern light pollution): 'The sea is agitated by the winds; but the aether is clear and open, without wind or any resistance.' I remembered his words as I battled home along Otterspool Promenade, blown to bits by a strong north-westerly.

The local historian Richard Griffiths declared that Otterspool Station had been built on the site of what had originally been Lower Lodge in King John's ancient Toxteth Park. What is certain is that Jeremiah Horrocks was born in a farmhouse within Toxteth Park in 1618. At the age of fourteen he went up to Emmanuel College, Cambridge, with the intention of entering the Church. His real passion, however, was for astronomy, and in Cambridge he was able to read the works of Ptolemy, Copernicus, Tycho Brahe and Kepler.

Horrocks' nightly observations of the skies did not fit with the established astronomical tables. He made an accurate prediction of the transit of Venus across the face of the sun and this he observed from the village of Hoole, near Preston.*

Sharp observation revealed to Horrocks that Saturn and Jupiter were not where Kepler had predicted them to be, and he rightly concluded that these great planets influenced each other as to their positions. He went on to indicate that the moon's orbit was influenced by the sun as well as by the earth. All this he discovered before his premature death at the age of twenty-three. It was fifty years later that Sir Isaac Newton acknowledged his debt to Horrocks, as did Halley, who wrote,

> that alone of our Horrocks which attributes to the moon's orbit a libratory motion of the apsides, and a variable eccentricity, seems to approach the truth of nature; for it represents the diameters more agreeably to observation, and shows her motion more accurately than any other hypothesis which I have hitherto seen.'

---

* By remarkable coincidence, Venus crossed the face of the sun again in the summer of 2004 as I was sitting in the Cambridge University library, working on this book.

Herschel summed up his achievement as 'the pride and boast of British astronomy.'

Sadly, the majority of the citizens of Liverpool have never heard of Jeremiah Horrocks, but part of his achievement is inscribed in stone at the Ancient Chapel.

This Tablet is erected to the memory of Jeremiah Horrox, who foretold, and was the first to observe the transit of Venus across the sun's disc on November 24th, 1641. He also made other valuable discoveries in astronomy.

He was born in Toxteth Park, near Otterspool, about 1618, and died there January 3rd, 1641.

It is believed that before going to Cambridge he was a pupil of the Rev. Richard Mather, the first minister of this Chapel, and that within its precincts he was buried.

The interior of the Ancient Chapel of Toxteth, where Richard Mather preached and in which he may have taught Jeremiah Horrocks before he went up to Cambridge.

AUTHOR

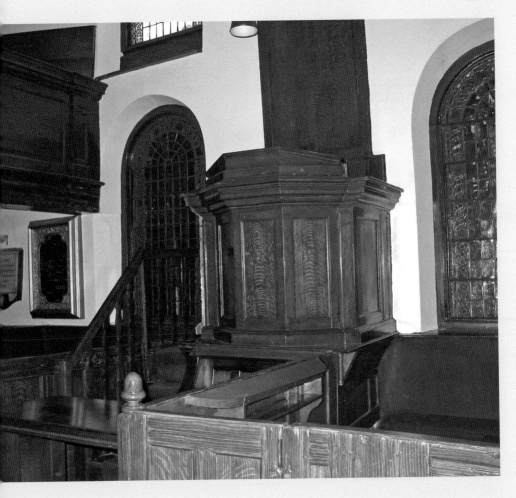

55

The entire Liverpool landscape has changed since the time of Jeremiah Horrocks, but he would certainly have recognised the sky and a winter sunset such as this over the Mersey near to the house where he was born.
AUTHOR

SIX

'One of the Wonders of Britain'

LIVERPOOL had not one but two royal beginnings. King John's foundation of the borough in 1207 was the first, and the restoration of the monarchy in 1660 was the second. Not that Charles II did anything dramatic about the little northern town, but rather that, for various reasons, at long last the fortunes of Liverpool appeared to be more secure. The seventeenth century had begun with Liverpool's population at little more than 1,000 and ended with one of 5,000. The seven streets of the medieval borough were to prove totally inadequate, and the town began to spread beyond the bounds of its medieval foundation.

Liverpool's good fortune is not unconnected with the capital's misfortunes. In two successive years London was devastated: by the Great Plague of 1665, and then by the Great Fire of 1666. Pepys' Diary gives us first-hand record of these twin devastations.

16 October 1665   But Lord, how empty the streets are and melancholy, so many poor sick people in the streets full of sores; and so many sad stories overheard as I walk, every body talking of this dead, and that man sick, and so many in this place, and so many in that. And they tell me that in Westminster there is never a physician and but one apothecary left, all being dead; but that there are great hopes of a decrease this week; God send it!

2 September 1666   ... saw the fire grow; and as it grew darker, appeared more and more, and in corners and upon steeples and between churches and houses, as far as we could see up the hill of the City, in a most horrid malicious bloody flame ... It made me weep to see it.

The fire burned on for four days, and four-fifths of the area of the old walled city was totally destroyed.

Quite unconnected with the horrors of plague and fire was a trading venture that set out from Liverpool in 1666. A small sailing vessel, The *Antelope*, set out from the Liver Pool with £200 worth of cargo and crossed the Atlantic to Barbados. When she returned safely to the Mersey in the following August with a cargo of sugar cane, the profits were equal to twice the investment. Encouraged by the success of the trip, and tempted by the lure of heavy profits, within a decade there were a dozen ships on the Barbados run, while others began to trade with mainland America and to transport tobacco.

At this time, Bristol was, after London, the most important seaport in England, but as Liverpool's transatlantic trade began to grow, a number of merchants decided to relocate their businesses from London to the north-western port, well away from hostile Dutch and French vessels in the English Channel. Also important was the fact that the greatly expanding textile industry around Manchester needed a port through which to export its goods, and by this time Liverpool had no opposition from Chester. By 1673 one Richard Blome reported his observations of Liverpool where 'diverse eminent merchants, whose trade and traffic, especially with the West Indies, make it famous.' In 1668 the landowner Sir Edward Moore negotiated over a piece of land in Dale Street with

> *Mr Smith, a great sugar baker from London, a man as report says, worth £40,000; and according to agreement, he is to build all the front twenty-seven yards, a stately house of good hewn stone four stories high, and then to go through the same building with a large entry; and there on the back side, to erect a house for boiling and drying sugar, otherwise called a sugar baker's house. The pile of building must be forty feet square and four stories high, all of hewn stone'*

Liverpool became the cane importing and sugar refining capital of the country.*

The tobacco trade became even more important than the sugar trade, and caused Sir Thomas Johnson to declare in 1701, 'We are sadly envied, God knows, especially the tobacco trade, at home and abroad.'

Some new streets were built within the framework of the old seven streets of King John's Liverpool – for example Fenwick Street, Preeson's Row, Lancelot's Hey, Sir Thomas Street and others. Possibly the most significant development

---

* Years later, the Tate & Lyle empire was centred in Liverpool, and remained a vital element in the economy until the latter part of the twentieth century.

was made by Lord Molyneux, who established a road from the castle down through the orchards, to the Pool. He gave it his own name, which was soon contracted to Lord Street. The street was important because it headed towards the land over the Pool – the waste or the heath as it was known – and which was claimed by the burgesses as their territory for development.

The original building donated by John Crosse to be the Exchange and Town Hall had come to the end of its useful life and was demolished. A new stone building, 'the first great public building erected in Liverpool' was built in the market area which stands just to the south of the present Town Hall. Like its medieval predecessor, there was a covered area below and council chamber and banqueting hall above. It was commented upon very favourably by visitors to the city early the following century.

By the end of the century, the size of the population demanded that Liverpool become a parish in its own right rather than being dependent upon St Mary's in nearby Walton. And Liverpool's population had far outgrown the capacity of the chapel of Saint Nicholas. The burgesses petitioned Parliament to remedy their problem:

> It was formerly a small fishing town, but many people coming from London in time of the sickness and after the fire, several ingenious men settled in Liverpool, which caused them to trade to the plantations and other places, which occasioned sundry tradesmen to come and settle there, which hath so enlarged their trade, that from scarce paying the salary of the officers of the customs, it is now the third port of the trade of England, and pays upwards of £50,000 per annum to the king; and by reason of such increase many new streets are built, and still in building; and many gentlemen's sons of the counties of Lancaster, Yorkshire, Derbyshire, Staffordshire, Cheshire, and North Wales, are put apprentices in the town …

A new church, St Peter's, was established over the Pool, on the waste; the building gave its name to Church Street. Having lacked parish status for 500 years, Liverpool suddenly had two parish churches and two rectors, Rev. Robert Stythe and Rev. W. Atherton. St Peter's survived in use until after the First World War and before its demolition it was recorded for posterity in black and white photographs.

In his monumental history of the town, Sir James Picton summed up the immense growth and development of the town within one century:

> The commencement of the century found it a quiet medieval appendage to the duchy and the neighbouring lords, not only not progressive but decayed and decaying. The close of the century left it a thriving, busy, prosperous town, with

An engraving made from the Peters' painting in 1680. Some of the buildings are easier to see than they are in the painting.

all the elements of business and commerce in full activity and progress. Half a millennium had passed since the charter of John, but it might be truly said that the last forty years had made more progress than the preceding four centuries and a half.

As the seventeenth century led into the eighteenth, Liverpool was visited by two intrepid travellers, who have both left invaluable written evidence of their visits. Celia Fiennes visited the town in 1698, and Daniel Defoe made several visits between 1680 and 1715. Miss Fiennes rode across the Wirral from Burton and took the ferry across the Mersey:

I ferry'd over and was an hour and a half in the passage; it's of great breadth and at low water is so deep and salt as the sea almost, though it does not cast so green a hew on the water as the sea, but else the waves toss and the rocks great all round it and is as dangerous as the sea; its in a sort of Hoy that I ferried over and my horses, the boat would have held 100 people.

Defoe also entered the town from the river, and his account of how he came ashore is interesting and indicated just how much had to be done before there could be easy movement of passengers or cargo from ship to shore:

Here is a ferry over the Mersey, which, at full sea, is more than two miles over. We land on the flat shore on the other side, and are contented to ride through the water for some length, not on horseback but on the shoulders of some honest Lancashire clown, who comes knee deep to the boat side, to truss you up, and then runs away with you, as nimbly as you desire to ride, unless his trot were easier; for I was shaken by him that had the luck to be carried by more than I car's for, and much worse than a hard trotting horse would have shaken me.

Celia Fiennes was impressed by what she saw in the little town, and her account is very valuable in giving us some idea about the changed face of Liverpool at an important point in its transformation from remote medieval borough to world-famous seaport.

Liverpool which is in Lancashire is built just on the river Mersey, mostly new built houses of brick and stone after the London fashion; the first original was a few fishermen's houses and now is grown to a large fine town and but a parish and one church, though there be 24 streets in it; there is indeed a little chapel and there are a great many Dissenters in the town; it is a very rich trading town the houses of brick and stone built high and even, that a street quite through looks very handsome, the streets well pitched; there are abundance of persons well dressed and of good fashion; the streets are faire and long, its London in miniature as much as ever I saw anything; there is a very

Always referred to as 'the Peters' painting', this is the earliest painting of Liverpool to have survived. The parish church, the Tower, the Castle and the Exchange are the most prominent buildings.
LIVERPOOL MARITIME MUSEUM

pretty Exchange stands on 8 pillars all of stone and its railed over which is very handsome town hall; over all is a tower and cupola that is so high that from thence one has the whole view of the town and the country round; in a clear day you may see the Isle of Man.

Not long before St Peter's church was demolished, one rector judged it to be 'cramped and undistinguished', yet when Defoe visited it on his third visit to Liverpool, he was impressed with it, standing as it then was, surrounded by fields, and he described it as 'a noble large building all of stone, well-finished; has in it a fine font of marble placed in the body of the church, surrounded by a beautiful iron pallisado.' There was a peal of eight bells in the tower.

Defoe also commented most favourably on the town's developments over the period of his visits:

Liverpool is one of the wonders of Britain, and that more, in my opinion, than any of the wonders of the Peak; the town was, at my first visiting it, about the year 1680, a large, handsome, well built and increasing or thriving town; at my second visit, anon 1690, it was much bigger than at my first seeing it, and, by the reports of the inhabitants, more than twice as big as it was twenty years before that; but, I think, I may safely say that at this my third seeing it, for I was surprised at the view, it was more than double what it was at the second; and, I am told, that it still visible increased both in wealth, people, business, and buildings. What it may grow to in time, I know not.

In a word, there is no town in England, London excepted, that can equal Liverpool for the fineness of its streets and the beauty of the buildings; many of the houses are of free stone, and completely finished; and all the rest (of the new part I mean) of brick, and handsomely built as London itself.

From his uncomfortable first landing at Liverpool, Defoe was conscious of 'the particular disadvantage of a flat shore', which did not provide adequate facilities for loading and unloading.

This exposed the merchants to great difficulties in their business; for though the harbour was good, and the ships rode well in the offing, yet they were obliged to ride there as in a road rather than a harbour. Here was no mole or haven to bring in their ships and lay them up, (as the seamen call it) for the winter; and no key for the delivering of goods ...

Today the Mersey shore around Liverpool is now almost totally man-made. With container base, dry and wet docks, floating landing stage and riverside promenade, it is not easy to visualise what the shoreline was like before it was modified so drastically. However, there are a few visual hints to trigger the imagination. The Mersey does not have a steeply sloping shore and at places such as Rock Ferry and Eastham in the Wirral, and near to Otterspool in Liverpool, low tides can reveal what the shoreline must have been like. To disembark from a Mersey ferry boat at low tide to be faced with a steeply sloping walkway up to the Pier Head is to be made aware of huge tidal variations on the Mersey. The Pool was no more than a tidal creek, and vessels must frequently have been left at undignified angles in the mud at low tide. Conditions might have been satisfactory for the small coastal craft of previous centuries, but serious transatlantic traffic could not have been developed without some daring and imaginative civil engineering.

The River Mersey at low tide, revealing the gently sloping shore that was such an initial hindrance to the development of the town as a serious port. Daniel Defoe remembered vividly how he was transported from ship to shore by a man who picked him up and carried him.
AUTHOR

The interior of St Peter's church in Church Street. The church was used as a temporary cathedral after the foundation of the diocese.

SEVEN
On the Map

A VERY SIGNIFICANT document survives from 1725: the first authoritative map of Liverpool. 'The Mapp of all the Streets Lanes and Alleys within the Town of Liverpool with one side of the River Mersey layd down by a scale of 80 yds to an inch. J. Chadwick 1725.' The population in 1700 was estimated at about 5,000; by 1750 this had risen to 18,000, and ten years later to 25,000. The town was expanding rapidly, and we are very fortunate that the physical growth has been recorded by several competent map makers: Chadwick was followed by Eyes in 1765, and by Perry in 1768.

It is the fate of economically vibrant towns that their fabric is frequently and often totally renewed. From this period, however, we are able to find some buildings that are still standing today. The old pattern of streets from the medieval period is still discernible on the maps, as it is today, but unfortunately very little of Georgian Liverpool survives. The townspeople must have felt relieved when in 1704 they were able to acquire the lease on the castle, now in a hopeless state of disrepair. When they were eventually able to demolish it in 1725 the last shadow of Molyneux domination was shifted from their minds as well as from their skyline. Then, in 1737, they purchased the Tower from the Stanley family, although it was not demolished for another hundred years. The parish church of Our Lady and St Nicholas survived from the fourteenth century, although the walls were demolished and rebuilt in 1774, but even that building is not the one we know today. St Peter's in Church Street survived into the days of black and white photography but it was demolished in 1922 and remembered now only with a brass cross set into a pavement on the site.

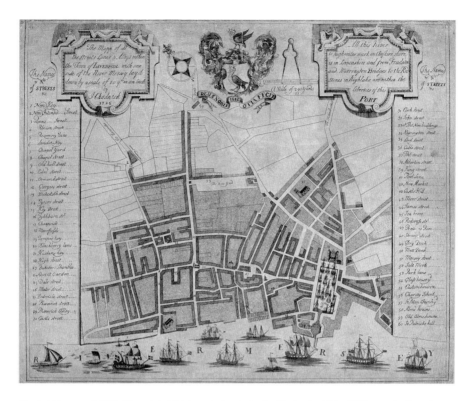

Chadwick's map of 1725. The original H-shaped street plan is still clearly visible. If this map is viewed alongside a current map of the city, the small size of the town during the early decades of the eighteenth century is clear. The most significant feature on this map is the Dock, seen here packed with ships.

However, a stone's throw from St Peter's stands Liverpool's oldest building, now known as Bluecoat Chambers. It is described by Quentin Hughes as 'the ancient gem of Liverpool'. Building started in 1717 and had been completed by the time Chadwick's map was drawn in 1725. It was badly damaged during the Second World War, but has undergone careful restoration and rebuilding.

Before the middle of the eighteenth century, Liverpool's second town hall was suffering from structural problems. As well as being too small, the pillars on which it rested had started to sink. John Wood the Younger* was engaged to design a new building appropriate to the increasing size and wealth of the town, and the foundation stone was laid on 14 September 1749.

---

* John Wood and his father were also responsible for such Georgian masterpieces as Bath's Circus, Queen Square and the Royal Crescent. It was a sign of Liverpool's success that it attracted an architect of such fame.

The gentlemen of the Common Council, in their gowns, attended Mr. Mayor to the hall; and the corporate body from thence, about one o'clock at noon, went in procession, with their regalia and officers, with music preceding them to the new work, where the Worshipful Joseph Clegg, Esq., mayor, addresses himself to the burgesses in handsome speech on the occasion, and struck down and laid the first stone of the noble work, and gave the workmen money on the occasion, which example was followed by the rest of the Council and merchants present, and was proclaimed by the loud huzzas of all the vast concourse of freemen and others present.

When the building was completed in 1745, there was a week of civic rejoicing … The exterior of the building we see today is largely the work of John Wood, but after a disastrous fire in the winter of 1795, the interior was completely redesigned by James Wyatt with the assistance of John Foster. The Corinthian portico of the front entrance was a new feature, together with a more effective dome surmounted a raised drum admitting light to the interior. Even the 1745 building must have been enormously impressive and must have done much for the confidence of the rapidly developing borough.

Several famous visitors came to the town and were impressed with their experiences. In 1755 the Methodist John Wesley, having preached in Manchester and Warrington,

went on to Liverpool, one of the neatest, best-built towns I have seen in England. I think it is full twice as large as Chester; most of the streets are quite straight. Two thirds of the town, we are informed, have been added within these forty years. If it continues to increase in the same proportion, in forty years more it will nearly equal Bristol. The people in general are the most mild and courteous I ever saw in a seaport town …

Bucks' view of Liverpool, showing the jetty that was built out into the estuary from the Dock entrance.

67

Saint Peter's church, which gave its name to Church Street. Defoe admired the building but the twentieth century demolished it. From 1885 to 1910 the building functioned as the pro-cathedral. It was wholly unsuitable as a cathedral, but its demolition was an example of Liverpool's architectural vandalism.

Samuel Derrick of Bath visited in 1760 also commented favourably on the residents, whom he found to be 'friendly to strangers, even to those of whom they have the least knowledge, their tables are plenteously furnished and their viandes well served up …' On Liverpool's waterfront, he said:

> The docks are flanked by broad commodious quays surrounded by handsome brick houses, inhabited for the most part by seafaring people, and communicating with the town by drawbridges and floodgates, which a man must be wary in crossing over, as they are pretty narrow.

The Liverpool merchants and ship owners were well aware of the natural disadvantages of their shoreline. With a vast tidal range and muddy banks, they were only able to load and unload at certain states of the tide. To be sure, Liverpool was better placed than Chester, as we have seen, and the tortuous river Avon was a much greater obstacle to shipping for Bristol than the Mersey was to Liverpool, but the merchants would have been very keen to find a solution.

On one of the few clear blue days of a wet and dreary February, I decided to set out to walk parts of the Mersey shore. I wanted to see Liverpool from 'over the water', the Wirral, so I approached the shoreline at high tide near Eastham, where mature woodland grows right down to the water's edge. From the Wirral shore the basin of the river shortly after high tide was vast, and the water's edge was thick with birds and even to my untutored eye there were several breeds of duck, dunlin, curlew and geese flying overhead. I then walked the granite and concrete of the Liverpool shoreline from Otterspool along to Pier Head to view the river when the tide was out and I tried to imagine the problems faced by seamen before the construction of the docks. Acres of muddy sand extend from

THE EXCHANGE .(NOW THE TOWN HALL)
as it was before the Fire in 1795.

what had been the entrances to the old south docks down to the water line. At low tide the old Pool must have been little more than a modest stream draining down from the Moss Lake and the sailing vessels would have sat at rakish angles in the mud. Without some way of coping with the levels of the river at low tide, Liverpool had no future as a seaport in the modern world.

Before Defoe's final visit to the town a most daring and pioneering decision was taken to remedy the situation. In 1708 an application was made to Parliament to drain the ancient Liver Pool and to construct within its mouth the first commercial wet dock in the world, one hundred yards wide and two hundred yards long and protected from the ebb tide by massive gates. The final plans and the oversight of the whole enterprise were the responsibility of the young civil engineer Thomas Steers. These modifications to the Mersey shoreline can well be regarded as the most dramatic and significant development in the whole history of the port. It was a massive engineering task for the times, hampered by tides, but in one way made easier in that it was being built up out of the Pool rather than excavated from dry land. Evidence of the construction of what became known as the Old Dock was revealed by an archaeological dig in 2001, when parts of the brick and sandstone structure were photographed. More extensive explorations were carried out in 2004. The Old Dock is claimed to be the oldest wet dock in the world though a much smaller development at Rotherhithe on the Thames was of a similar date. Defoe approved. This way of working set the pattern for much future shoreline development, during which dock development was on land reclaimed from the river.

By Defoe's final visit to Liverpool he was able to comment on the massive improvements that had been made:

> The inhabitants and merchants have, of late years, and since the visible increase of their trade, made a large basin or wet dock, at the east end of the town, where, at an immense charge, the place considered, they have brought the tide from the Mersey to flow by an opening that looks to the south, and the ships go in north, so that the town entirely shelters it from the westerly and northerly winds, the hills from the easterly, and the ships lye, as in a mill-pond, with the utmost safety and convenience. As this is so great a benefit to the town, and that the like is not to be seen anywhere in England but here, I mean London excepted, it is well worth the observation and imitation of many other trading places in Britain who want such a convenience, and, for want of it, lose their trade.

A small tidal basin was created outside the dock gates, and in 1734 a new dock to be known later as Salthouse Dock was excavated to handle the exports of the

Cheshire salt trade. The importance of the new dock development to the future commercial importance of the town is reflected in the number of ships owned by Liverpool men, and by the number of sailors. In 1700 there were 70 ships and about 800 seamen. By 1751 the respective numbers had more than trebled, to 220 and 3,319.

Liverpool had always been on the fringes of Lancashire. Now increasing maritime trade caused the town to face seawards more and more. From its earliest days, Liverpool's inland communications had always been poor, with low-lying marshy land to the east discouraging attempts to construct a decent road. Westwards from Warrington, the only means of transport into Liverpool was by horse-back or pack-horse. The nearest coach road was at Warrington. The construction of decent roads to Prescot and, more importantly, to Warrington were important for the town's development. The first stage coach service to London was started as late as 1761, the journey taking four days. Within five years this had been reduced to three days in the winter and two in the summer. Even more important than roads for the carriage of bulky and heavy goods was the improvement to transport by water, and the early years of the century also saw the beginnings of the revolution in canal transport.

In 1720 Thomas Steers had been responsible for deepening the channel of the river Douglas so that coal could be transported by water from the coal mines around Wigan to the Douglas' confluence with the river Ribble and thence by sea to Liverpool. In 1722 an act was passed for the deepening of the Mersey and Irwell towards Manchester. Later the Weaver was made navigable to Nantwich, and the transportation of Cheshire salt became easier and cheaper. In 1755 legislation was passed to improve the Sankey Brook to transport coal from the mines near St Helens directly to the Mersey. Engineer Brindley judged that the Brook was too narrow and winding for the deepening of the channel to be of much use. Instead, he simply used the flow of water to feed the very first artificially created canal, or 'navigation' as it was called, in England, the Sankey Navigation, which was opened in 1759.

CANALS

As I watch a container lorry rumble along the Dock Road, I cannot help but surmise how many pack horses early in the eighteenth century would have been needed to shift the same weight and volume of goods. Where possible, of course, bulk goods such as the proverbial coals from Newcastle, were handled by riverborne or seagoing shipping. Liverpool's seagoing trade was booming, but its inland waterway links needed to be improved too. Thomas Steers was again called upon, this time to survey the existing natural waterways; there was great support for a navigation involving the Mersey and the Irwell so that barges could be drawn to and from Manchester, but it never became a very successful waterway.

The Sankey Brook near Newton-le-Willows.
AUTHOR

The Sankey/St Helens Canal with original stonework in perfect condition, part of the country's first wholly man-made canal.

AUTHOR

Much of the countryide near the canal was blighted by industry and the dumping of waste materials but by the end of the twentieth century the canal and the adjacent land have been cleared and redeveloped for recreational purposes.

AUTHOR

In its day, the Manchester Ship Canal was a vital waterway that could admit even ocean-going vessels right through to Manchester.
AUTHOR

A stretch of the Leeds and Liverpool Canal in Liverpool, once a very busy route for raw materials and manufactured goods.
AUTHOR

Coal was one commodity carried by the early waterways. It was already shipped from Wigan to Liverpool via the rivers Douglas and Ribble. Then the engineers Henry Berry and John Ashton were commissioned to survey the Sankey Brook with an eye to converting it into a 'navigation' so that it too could carry coal to Liverpool and beyond. It was clear to them that the waters were inadequate for a successful navigation, and so, in some secrecy, work began to cut a canal, which would be fed by the water from the brook. The new waterway, completed in 1757, eventually called the Sankey/St Helens Canal was the first genuine man-made canal in the country, another first for the people of Merseyside.

The age of canal building was hectic, and the trade carried by these new waterways was very important for Liverpool. A number of new connections, including the Bridgewater, extended the network significantly. Roads continued to be very important, but in the realm of bulk transport, canals reigned supreme for more than half a century.

There followed a scheme of major importance: a hugely ambitious plan to link Liverpool, across the Pennines, with Leeds. Despite several changes of mind over the route to be followed, the eventual canal passed through many of the newly industrialised towns including Wigan (with its coal supplies), Blackburn, Burnley, Skipton, Keighley and Leeds itself. The 127 miles of excavation started from Halsall in 1770, although the final connection across the Pennines was not made until 1816. Not until 1846 was the logical destination of the canal achieved, when at last the barges were able to float right down to the Liverpool docks themselves, via the Stanley Dock.

Almost half a century later came the building on one final, great waterway, the very thought of which filled the Liverpool merchants and authorities with dismay. For decades all of the bales of raw cotton and then the finished cloth and garments – the very foundations of the Manchester and Lancashire economy – had to pass through Liverpool's docks and pay duties to the port. Not surprisingly, the Manchester merchants sought to avoid the cost and lack of control which Liverpool's dominance of maritime trade implied. Liverpool tried to block the scheme, but approval was given for a direct link from Manchester to the sea, the Manchester Ship Canal. The canal did not even pass through Liverpool, and ships joined the waterway at Eastham on the Wirral shore. It opened to shipping on New Year's Day 1894. Liverpool's economy did not, in fact, suffer as had been feared even though, in its heyday, the ship canal was very busy.

With the increase in size of vessels, even such a prestigious canal lost its importance before the end of the twentieth century. Just as the South Docks at Liverpool became outmoded, so eventually did the ship canal. At Salford Quays, the ship canal's terminus has also been remodelled for modern times.

THE OLD DOCK

In the modest, early days of the port the Liver Pool had proved to be a useful little shelter, out of the fierce tides of the river, but by the beginning of the eighteenth century it was totally inadequate. In 1699 there had been proposals to dredge the Pool. Then, in 1703, fierce winds and storms led Sir Thomas Johnson MP to seek engineering advice on the possible improvement of the port facilities. A leading engineer of the day, George Sorogold, was duly consulted, and he produced plans for draining the Pool; his proposals were rejected by Parliament and when the rejections were later over-ruled Sorogold was too busy to accept the commission. Through the agency of the Earl of Derby, Thomas Steers was appointed Dock Engineer, and he arrived in Liverpool in May 1710.

Not much is known of his early life apart from the fact that he was born in Kent, probably in 1672. He must have been well educated as is made clear by the grasp of mathematics revealed by his notes and calculations. The Army List of July 1702 recorded that he was a quartermaster with the King's Own 4th Regiment of Foot. Because of his engineering interest, he might well have been involved in surveying and excavation work in Holland, where hydraulic engineering skills were well advanced because so much land lay below sea level. When he returned to

Before the massive building programme for the Grosvenor Project was under way, Oxford Archaeology North were able to undertake an extensive dig which revealed brick and stone from the walls of the Old Dock. At the bottom of their trenches, in the old Pool, the tide still came in and out.
OXFORD ARCHAEOLOGY

England and married, his father-in-law gave the newly-weds some property in Rotherhithe on the south bank of the Thames, where dock excavations had already started.

In Liverpool Steers produced plans which were quite novel, possibly derived from observations in Holland. He was the designer for the project but also the contractor for the excavations. Instead of excavating a dock, his plan was to construct the dock within the basin of the Pool behind great gates to hold back the waters of the dock when the tide was low. It was an immense project using brick and stone to construct a dock two hundred yards long and one hundred yards wide.

The dock was a major and pioneering feat. Oxford Archaeology North undertook excavations in 2001 which uncovered dressed sandstone blocks, hand-made bricks and even

Part of Liverpool One below which the remains of the Old Dock are covered forever.

ELIZABETH KENNERLEY

some of the timberwork. A more extensive dig in 2004 was able to find evidence for the full extent of the dock walls. The Old Dock, as it became known, was crucial not just for the development of the docks in Liverpool but throughout the country – a first for Liverpool in civil engineering. Although it was opened in 1715, work continued until 1721.

A second bill went through parliament in 1717 which gave authority for a dry dock to be constructed between the Old Dock and the river. In the same year Steers was appointed Dock Master. In 1738 he began work on a new dock of 23,000 square yards, three times the size of the original dock. Because of the main material which it handled, this new South Dock has always been called Salthouse Dock. Steers died in 1750, and the final work on Salthouse was overseen by a young engineer called Henry Berry who was to be responsible for the Sankey Canal – another world first.

Steers' standing in the town rose steadily. He was made a freeman in 1713, and four years later he was elected to the Town Council. Later he became a bailiff and rose to the position of mayor in 1739. He died in Liverpool and was buried in St Peter's churchyard on 2 November 1750.

BLUECOAT CHAMBERS

Bluecoat Chambers on School Lane is the oldest surviving building in central Liverpool. When the visitor walking down busy Bold Street and into Church Street turns left down Church Alley, the building straight ahead speaks of an age long gone. The architect is not known, but the quality and importance of the building are beyond question, its history remarkably well recorded, partly because for nearly two hundred years it was the home of the Blue Coat School. Building was started in 1717 and completed in 1725.

The school owes its origins to two men: Rev. Robert Styth, one of the two rectors of the newly established parish of Liverpool, and Bryan Blundell, master mariner and part-owner of a trading vessel called the *Mulberry*. During Blundell's

Bluecoat Chambers (1725) is the oldest remaining building within the old town boundaries. Though severely damaged by bombs in the Second World War, it was faithfully restored and provides a quiet haven close to the busy crowds of shoppers in nearby Church Street.
AUTHOR

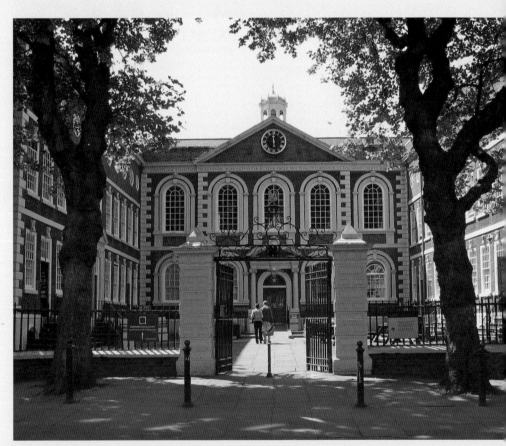

absence at sea in 1708, Styth applied to the council for 'a convenient piece of ground for building of a school for teaching poor children to read, write and cast accounts', and a small building was constructed for £35 in School Lane. After Styth's death in 1713, Blundell decided to give up the sea and devote himself to the charitable work of the school. Conditions for the poor in the town were so bad that Blundell realised that a day-school could not do enough, and so he planned a boarding school, the Blue Coat Hospital, in a much larger and more imposing building; by 1744 one hundred children, boys and girls, were being educated and cared for. So they might worship across the road in St Peter's church, a new gallery was erected at the west end of the building; there the children might 'stand, sit, kneel and hear divine service and sermons in the same'.

Blundell worked tirelessly up to his death in 1756 for the growth and development of his school, and much of his work is recorded for posterity in his own words. He was buried at Our Lady and Saint Nicholas, where his epitaph stood until the destruction of the church during the Second World War. After his death his work for the school was taken up by two of his sons in succession, and Jonathan, his youngest son, held the post of Treasurer for thirty-six years.

Early in the nineteenth century the state of the building was examined, and restoration was embarked upon with great care. The brickwork was 'to be pointed in an effective manner, but no alteration to be made to the front of the building so as to injure or affect its present appearance and general character'. The Earl of Sefton contributed new stone from his quarries in Toxteth Park. By the end of the century, although the building was well preserved, the conditions were cramped and inadequate for the future development of the school, which moved in May 1906 to impressive new buildings in Wavertree.

The school continues to flourish in yet further new buildings on the Wavertree site, while the original building remains an important part of the city heritage as a Grade 1 listed building. In 1913 it was bought by Lord Leverhulme for use as an arts centre, a plan that was upset by the war. In 1927 the building was bought by the Bluecoat Arts Society. Several artists, including the potter Julia Carter Preston, have had their studios there. There are a number of small specialist shops and, particularly in the summer, the courtyard at the front and the gardens at the rear are filled with people enjoying the sun in a beautiful environment.

In 2005 the building was closed and shrouded as it was renovated, and a new 2,250-square metre extension added. Interestingly, the architects engaged to do the work discovered that there were 32 different floor levels in the old building, which must have presented them with all sorts of problems! In any event, £12.5 million and three years later, on 15 March 2008, Bluecoat was re-opened, complete with splendid new exhibition areas with better accessibility. The new extension is built mainly in brick to link with the old building, although it has a copper roof and more modern materials internally. It houses a multi-purpose performance area, four galleries, several small retail outlets, artists' studios, a café and a restaurant, and a very pleasant courtyard.

The Grand Turk is a modern reconstruction of an eighteenth-century man of war. The masts and rigging in the evening sunlight give some idea of the dock skyline in the eighteenth and nineteenth centuries. AUTHOR

EIGHT

'Obscurity to Celebrity ... Poverty to Wealth'

W
HAT WAS HAPPENING at sea, particularly in the
Atlantic, was of crucial importance for the development of one of
the great seaports of the world. Trade with the West Indies and
America continued, but some vast fortunes were made by less honourable
means, and one book on Liverpool begins a chapter of eighteenth-century
developments 'Sugar, Plunder and Slaves'. Disagreements with Spain over trade
through its colonial ports in Mexico and Cuba led to some very profitable
smuggling, and by 1757 there were 106 Liverpool ships involved, with annual
profits in the region of £250,000.

By 1739 England was at war with Spain and five years later also with France.
Far from limiting the earning capacity of Liverpool vessels, there was even more
money to be made, this time from privateering. During war, ships could be
licensed to attack and capture enemy vessels, in some instances making vast
fortunes very quickly. One such was Fortunatus Wright; born in Wallasey, son
of a Liverpool mariner, he set out in the *Fame* and captured no fewer than
sixteen French ships, in all worth about £400,000. William Hutchinson was
famous in Liverpool maritime circles particularly for his command of the
Liverpool when one successful attack yielded profits of £20,000. In 1778 Peter
Baker had built a ship called the *Mentor* which appeared so unseaworthy that
no one would buy her so, to the derision of other ship-masters, he set out to sea
himself. When he attacked and captured the *Carnatic*, he earned for himself a
fortune of £135,000 and built a large house on the slopes of Mossley Hill which

people nicknamed Carnatic Hall; to this day the name is kept alive by a road and a university hall of residence.

Not all privateering was successful, and many Liverpool vessels were lost. The town itself was seen to be under great threat when in 1759 Monsieur Thurot and a small squadron of French vessels swept into the Irish Sea to the consternation of the townspeople, who went to great lengths to defend their town:

> *This week upwards of 70 heavy cannon have been mounted on the platforms, and several hundred men employed in completing them.*

During some of the earlier periods of her development, the majority of the people of Liverpool probably had little knowledge of international affairs and war between nations, but before the end of the eighteenth century Liverpool was the second port in the land, entirely dependent on sea-borne trade and sensitive to international tensions and aggression. Eighteenth-century England suffered more severely from the results of war than ever before in its history. In the words of Ramsey Muir:

> *The period from 1756 to 1815 is a period of almost continuous wars – wars the most gigantic ever waged in the history of England, perhaps in the history of the world. For they set every part of the globe aflame, Europe, America, Africa, India; and, above all, every sea echoed to the guns of battleships or privateers, and the unarmed trader was never safe except in great convoys.*

During the Seven Years War in the middle of the eighteenth century, Liverpool trade suffered, but privateering went on: and because one-third of the profits from a capture were divided among the crew, Liverpool vessels were rarely short of sailors, despite the constant aggression of the press-gang. By the Treaty of Paris at the end of the Seven Years War in 1763, there was expansion of the empire and in the words of Roy Strong, 'Britain now ruled the greatest empire since the Roman'. Liverpool was of crucial importance in the trading life of that empire, but there were growing signs of future problems on the other side of the Atlantic, leading in 1775 to the American War of Independence. Liverpool ships lay idle, crews were paid off, and as many as 3,000 sailors were thrown out of work; when ship owners tried to use the high levels of unemployment to reduce wages by a third, the sailors on one ship mutinied; others followed and riots and looting broke out in the town. Some of the boldest of the rioters brought cannon from the ships and began to bombard the town hall. Troops from Manchester had to be brought in to restore some order.

To make matters worse, in 1778 France declared war, and the following year was joined by Spain and Holland. The Liverpool privateers were once again spurred into action. As many as 120 vessels were prepared within just six months, and won £100,000 in the first five weeks. Thus, although Liverpool's official trade suffered badly during wartime, large sums continued to flow in to the port through the bravery and determination of the privateers.

The fortunes of the town, though temporarily dented as a result of the conflicts, continued to rise at this time through one trade that has not yet even been mentioned, although the present citizens remember it with shame. I have spoken recently to a man who recounted an incident relating to what can only be called the Liverpool myth. He is not the only one to have been taken near to the Pier Head before the Second World War to be shown, at the Goree Piazzas, the iron rings to which African slaves were chained. In fact, the slaves were not chained up in Liverpool, and very rarely did any come anywhere near the town. Liverpool, however, cannot deny the fact that its fame and fortune in the second half of the eighteenth century were founded at least in part upon the most evil trade in the world, in which men, women and children were captured in west Africa, chained together, shipped to the other side of the world and sold as slaves to the plantation owners in the West Indies and the southern states of America.

It is painful today even to acknowledge that Liverpool's wealth and civic pride derived in large measure to the vast fortunes that were generated by such an inhuman trade in human beings. In the eleven-year period from 1783, an astonishing 878 journeys were made by Liverpool slaving ships, in which 303,737 slaves were transported and sold for a total of £15,186,850. Even after all the expenses had been covered, £300,000 profit each year flowed into the town: and this was from only one leg of the triangular trading routes.

It might salve the modern conscience if it could be argued that the African trade owed its origins and success to the greed, immorality or insensitivity of a few evil men; but this was simply not the case. Biblical authority was called upon to condone, and even to encourage, this horrific treatment of the descendants of Ham, one of the three sons of Noah chronicled in the Old Testament of the Bible. An Act of Parliament passed in 1730 opened up the trade to allcomers for a registration fee of £2. Before the end of the nineteenth century, Sir James Picton passed judgement:

> It had flooded Liverpool with wealth, which invigorated every industry,
> provided the capital for docks, enriched and employed the mills of Lancashire,
> and afforded the means for opening out new and ever new lines of trade.
> Beyond a doubt it was the slave trade which raised Liverpool from a struggling
> port to be one of the richest and most prosperous trading centres of the world.

Everton in 1817. Eighteenth-century Everton was an attractive area to live in, away from the smoke, grime and disease of the tightly packed town. By the end of the nineteenth century the whole of the hill was covered in terraced houses. St George's church is the one feature remaining today.

At one time a quarter of the tonnage of the port was involved in the slave trade, engaged upon by over 100 of the most important merchants and hundreds of others who made smaller financial investments in the trade, as was recorded by a report in 1795:

> It is well known that many of the small vessels that import about a hundred slaves are fitted out by attorneys, drapers, ropers, grocers, tallow-chandlers, barbers, tailors, etc.

The trade route was triangular – beginning in west Africa, then to the West Indies and back to Liverpool – and profits could and were made on each of the passages. Manufactured goods from Manchester and the Midlands were much in demand on the coast of west Africa, where unscrupulous Africans raided villages, sometimes far inland in order to capture healthy inhabitants for sale into slavery. Whole families were taken, and the men immediately put in chains for the long trek to the coast. After the transactions at the coast, the 'cargo' were branded with hot irons, chained to each other, taken below decks and chained to the crowded wooden benches for the long passage. It was impossible for a tall person to stand upright because to save space there was only five feet eight inches headroom between decks.

John Newton is one of the best-known names associated with the trade, partly because of his extraordinarily chequered career at first aboard slaving vessels and later as an ordained minister in the Church of England. In 1788 he looked back on his experiences and wrote *Thoughts on the African Slave Trade*, in which he reported vividly on the horror of the conditions in which human beings were kept:

> *The cargo of a vessel of a hundred tons, or little more, is calculated to purchase from two hundred and twenty to two hundred and fifty slaves ... the Slaves lie*

St George's Dock basin cannot be found today because it was filled in to form the site for the Liver Building. This view in 1797 shows the parish church before the fatal collapse of the spire and tower.

in two rows, one above the other, like books on a shelf. I have known them so close, that the shelf would not easily contain one more ... the poor creatures, thus cramped for want of room, are likewise in irons, for the most part both hands and feet, and two together, which makes it difficult for them to turn or move, to attempt either to rise or lie down, without hurting themselves or each other ... The heat and smell of these rooms, when the weather will not admit of the slaves being brought upon deck, and of having their rooms cleaned every day, would be almost unsupportable to a person not accustomed to them ... They are kept down by the weather to breath a hot and corrupted air, sometimes for a week; this, adding to the galling of their irons, and the despondency which seizes their spirits when thus continued, soon becomes fatal. And every morning perhaps, more instances than one are found, of the living and the dead, like the Captives of Mezentius, fastened together.

When the weather permitted, batches of slaves, still in irons, were taken on to the deck, attached to another chain to prevent them from jumping over the side, and ordered to dance for exercise. The human cargo were at sea from between fifty to sixty days and if too many died, the profits suffered! Those who did survive were sold on, usually to plantation owners. For the third and final leg of the journey, the vessels were then loaded with sugar, tobacco and rum before returning to Liverpool. Most of the inhabitants of Liverpool might never have seen a black face (although a small number of slaves were brought over as house-servants), but surely all would have been aware of the trade.

It is not surprising that when a parliamentary bill for the abolition of the slave trade was supported by politicians such as Wilberforce, Pitt and Fox, the strongest opposition came from the Liverpool merchants, certain in their own minds that they would be ruined financially if the trade were ever to be suspended. However, Liverpool figures such as Rathbone and Roscoe were vehement in their support for abolition, and Rev. John Newton and Rev. John Yates both proclaimed their support from the pulpit. The Abolition Bill went through Parliament successfully in 1806; feelings ran high in Liverpool, but contrary to local fears, the end of the immoral trade did not lead to the collapse of the local economy.

At the start of the eighteenth century, the town's inhabitants had numbered about 5,000; by 1800 there were 77,653: the Georgian era had witnessed a population increase of over 1,500%. The year 1700 saw 102 ships through the port, in 1800 there were 4,746. The muddy tidal Pool of 1700 had given way to five docks as well as smaller basins and dry docks: twenty-six acres of safe water in total. The corporation's revenue in 1699 totalled £804 4s. 3d. and by 1800 it had rocketed a thousand-fold to £82,393 17s. 9d.

'LIVERPOOL AS IT WAS'

In 1853 Richard Brooke published a book entitled *Liverpool as it was during the last quarter of the eighteenth century 1775 to 1800*, 'the chief object of [which] is to preserve, unimpaired, the knowledge of various particulars and events relating to Liverpool, most of which would, perhaps otherwise soon have been forgotten'. Brooke was a fellow of the Society of Antiquaries at a time when there was keen interest in collecting and preserving information about the past. His father had arrived in Liverpool in 1776, and retained vivid memories of the town from one of the most formative periods in its history, a period of massive growth prior to its fame and glory in the nineteenth century. Almost everything he wrote about has now gone or been changed radically, but the 558 pages of his book are a great help to anyone attempting to visualise the town at this crucially formative period.

Although Celia Fiennes had written in glowing terms about the architectural excellence of Liverpool, Brooke (who had lived there all his life) was a little more discerning. 'In 1775, the interior of Liverpool presented to the eye little or nothing calculated to excite admiration or interest,' and the majority of the buildings were of 'dingy brick' and 'every street near the Town-hall was then narrow, irregular, and ill built,' and 'numerous dirty, confined, and mean courts and alleys were to be met with.' Although over five hundred years had passed since King John's charter, the town was still very small, and the town plan still dominated by the original seven streets.

Castle Street had always been one of the most important streets in the town, but Brooke described it as 'confined and ill built', and in some places it was so narrow 'that it was difficult that two carriages could pass at the same time'. Old Hall Street was 'ill built and dangerously narrow', and narrow was the adjective that he applied to most of the main streets of the town. Compared with today there was wide variety of use and function within small areas. For example, Pool Lane (modern South Castle Street) contained some large houses with respectable families as well as shops and small houses; Lord Street was very narrow, but had some good houses, 'tolerably good shops' and several taverns. What we know as Paradise Street and Whitechapel were then the Common Shore and Frog Lane and originally part of the upper stretches of the Pool. High tide and heavy downpours of rain caused regular flooding in this area.

Although we know that the main Liverpool streets had been paved from an early period, Brooke was critical of the state of the roads in his day, stating that 'the paving of the town was in a very objectionable state'. The pavements were made of cobble-stones 'set on end' which must have been impossible to keep clean and very uncomfortable for people walking on them. Only Clayton Square and Islington Flags were properly flagged, and it was 1799 before flagging was undertaken in Lord Street. The roadways themselves were little better, being 'paved in a rough and slovenly manner with large paving-stones'. Hackney carriages were in use by 1775, and when Castle Street had been widened, a stand for the carriages was established near to the Town Hall not far from a stand for sedan chairs.

Allerton Hall, mainly eighteenth-century but with early nineteenth-century additions, is still surrounded by pleasant parkland to the south of the city. For a time it was home of William Roscoe before his financial troubles.
AUTHOR

Movement about the streets after dark could be a dangerous activity, there being only infrequent oil lamps on the fronts of some of the houses. Brooke was scathing about the character and ability of most of the members of the watch: 'generally ignorant and inefficient – frequently men who were advanced in life, and inactive.' Brooke thought that their crying of the time and the weather throughout the night gave warning of their approach to the burglars and wakened the honest citizens who were in bed asleep.

The wretched state of the streets was exacerbated by the town's hopelessly inadequate sewerage system. Even many of the main streets had no sewers at all, and such as did exist were inadequate and poorly constructed. One of the frequent floods in Whitechapel in 1789 led to a number of residents moving out of their houses and being accommodated temporarily in the Infirmary.

The medieval townsfolk had drawn their fresh water from the Fall Well and carried it home themselves. Piped water was not a reality until the end of the eighteenth century. In the intervening years a system had been developed whereby horse-drawn water carts were trundled around the streets and delivered house to house.

Under the Improvement Act of 1786 the Liverpool Corporation Waterworks was established, but apparently did nothing until 1799 when the establishment of the Bootle Waterworks Company spurred the town into action, with the result that 1800 saw the laying of the first (wooden) water pipes.

WILLIAM ROSCOE

William Roscoe perhaps comes closest to the ideal of Renaissance Man than anyone else in Liverpool history: lawyer, art historian, bibliophile, art collector, poet, botanist, politician – the range of his interests and achievements was astonishing.

His origins were modest. He was born on 8 March 1753 at the Old Bowling Green House on Mount Pleasant, where his father was the publican. In his first year the family moved a short distance to a larger establishment with an extensive market-garden. Leaving school at twelve, he helped his father in the market-garden for three years before being articled to a solicitor. A friend, Francis Holden, began to teach him French, Latin and later Italian. One group of friends influenced him academically, and another spiritually – the group of Unitarians who met at what was to become Renshaw Street Chapel. In 1773 he was part of a group who established a Society for the Encouragement of the Arts, Painting and Design which the following year organised the first exhibition of painting ever held in Liverpool. Even though he never visited Italy (indeed, he hardly ever left Liverpool), he published in 1796 a highly influential *Life of Lorenzo de' Medici*, to be followed later by the biography of his son Pope Leo X

For a couple of years he lived at the Dingle. He was a founder of the Liverpool Athenaeum Club, which pre-dated the London club of the same name (and which still contains his library), and he helped establish the Liverpool Botanical Garden and gave the opening address in 1802. He was an active member of the West Derby Agricultural Society, and from 1792 he was engaged in a brave experiment to try to drain part of the notorious Chat Moss and to bring it into cultivation.

He was able to purchase Allerton Hall as a fitting setting for his growing family, art collection and library. Through his agricultural experiments he was invited to meet and stay with the famous Viscount Coke of Holkham Hall who was later to be invited to stay at Allerton.

He was known to be an ardent supporter of the abolition of slavery, and as an MP in 1806 he spoke in the House:

I have long resided in the town of Liverpool; for thirty years I have never ceased to condemn this inhuman traffic; and I consider it the greatest happiness of my existence to lift up my voice on this occasion against it, with the friends of justice and humanity.

William Roscoe – one of the most cultured and significant Liverpool figures.
WALKER ART GALLERY, NATIONAL MUSEUMS LIVERPOOL

Roscoe's opponents in Liverpool were the cause of actual physical violence when he returned to Liverpool, and he served only one term as member for Liverpool.

The year after abolition he published a hugely successful children's book *The Butterfly's Ball and the Grasshopper's Feast*, which sold 40,000 copies in its first year. Donald Macnaughton's biography of Roscoe lists 56 publications, from the four-volume *Life and Pontificate of Leo X* to single poems; from *Farm Leases in the Hundred of West Derby*, to *Monandrian Plants in the Order Scitamineae*, *chiefly drawn from living specimens at the Botanic Garden at Liverpool*; and from *A Selection of Psalms and Hymns* to *Observations on Penal Jurisprudence, and the Reformation of Criminals*.

The collapse of a bank with which he was associated led to the sale of Allerton Hall and many of his books and art treasures. He continued to write until his death despite the slight restrictions of strokes. He was a liberal reformer with a 'belief in progress, a humanist and humanitarian, maintaining a lively interest in and respect for individual human beings as well as human rights to a ripe old age.'

William Rathbone, with St George's Hall in the background.

Greenbank House, 1815, one-time home of the Rathbone family, is still beautifully preserved in gardens surrounding some of Liverpool University's halls of residence on the edge of Greenbank Park.

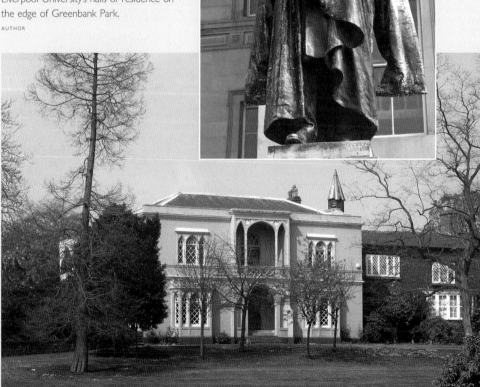

THE RATHBONE FAMILY
======

THE RATHBONE FAMILY

Peter Howell Williams in the Merseyside Civic Society's *Liverpolitana* is unequivocal in seeing the Rathbone family as the most influential family in Liverpool, 'No other family has so dominated Liverpool, each new generation adding to the lustre of the old.' As many as ten Rathbones were named William over a period of some 250 years, confusing for historians though not at the time!

William I was born in Cheshire and arrived in Liverpool in 1730 to open a sawmill before becoming a merchant and ship owner. His membership of the Society of Friends started the family tradition of nonconformity, although family allegiance was later transferred to the Unitarian movement. The second and third Williams were both founders of the Society for the Abolition of the Slave Trade, although William III was an astute trader and one of the first Englishman to import cotton from America, in 1784.

William IV was born in Liver Street off Park Lane in 1787, although a year later the family moved out of the town, for part of the year, to Greenbank, the family home for a hundred years before it became residential accommodation for Liverpool University. This William together with William V were to become Liverpool's greatest practical philanthropists during an age of devastating poverty and disease, Irish immigration and cholera epidemics. William IV laid the foundation stone of St George's Hall during his time as mayor and was active in much that led to the Municipal Reform Act of 1835. It was the Rathbone family who supported the work of the legendary Kitty Wilkinson in establishing the first public washhouse in the country. This remarkable lady and her achievements are commemorated in the Noble Women's Window in the Lady Chapel of Liverpool Cathedral.

When William V's wife was ill, she was nursed by Mary Robinson, whose care and skill so impressed William that he persuaded her, at his expense, to treat some of the Liverpool poor. This simple but practical beginning led eventually to the establishment of the District Nursing Society. Rathbone was aware of the deplorable state of nursing in the hospitals and knew that he needed practical advice if he were to help improve conditions, so in 1861 he wrote to Florence Nightingale. Her advice was to establish a school in Liverpool for the training of nurses: Rathbone followed her advice and established the Liverpool Training School and Home for Nurses. At the time there were over 1,000 people needing care and sustenance in the Liverpool Workhouse Infirmary and, after a year of negotiations, Rathbone and Florence Nightingale were responsible for the arrival of Agnes Jones and twelve trained nurses at the workhouse.

A female Rathbone, Eleanor, became the first woman councillor in Britain, in 1909. She went on to be elected as one of the first women MPs and to become the first woman minister in government. She was an important figure in the establishment of the School of Social Sciences at the University.

NINE

Cotton

I F T H E R E is one product more than any other which changed the skyscape for ever and was responsible for so many features and buildings which are a part of modern Liverpool, that product was American-grown cotton. Modest quantities of raw cotton had been imported through Liverpool from the West Indies, Brazil and India to supply the Lancashire textile trade,* but in the summer of 1784 an American sailing ship unloaded eight bags of raw cotton grown in America, imported by the Liverpool merchant William Rathbone and sold on to Jedediah Strutt & Company, one of Britain's most important cotton spinners, from Belper in Derbyshire.

During the Napoleanic Wars, France sold their colony of Louisiana, which included the Mississippi valley, to the USA, who began to develop the whole region until it became the most important cotton growing area in the world. At that time the colonists were not equipped to manufacture cotton cloth from the raw material, and so bales of raw cotton were transported across the Atlantic to the cotton manufacturers of north-west England, passing through the port of Liverpool, which also handled the export of the woven cloth to all parts of the world. Cotton has long been synonymous with Lancashire: trade in cotton was crucial to the commercial success of Lancashire's port, Liverpool. The first recorded local import of cotton from across the Atlantic was in 1758, when twenty-five bags were unloaded from Jamaica. By 1770, 5,521 bags were imported

---

* Liverpool's trade in textiles and raw materials in fact pre-dated cotton by centuries. Before cotton was widely used in the Lancashire textile industry, Irish linen had also made its way through Liverpool's docks.

from the West Indies. By 1820, half a million bales arrived annually in the port from America, and by 1850 this had risen a further threefold. At the end of the American War of Independence, Liverpool handled more American produce than any other port in the country. By 1795, 156 ships sailed to New York and 68 to Philadelphia at a time when Britain's largest port, London, handled only 36 to New York and 22 to Philadelphia.

The Atlantic trade was not the only territory to show steady growth at this period. Since 1600, all oriental trade had been monopolised by the East India Company, who had profited enormously after Clive's victories in India in 1757. In 1813 trade with India was opened to all, and twenty years later was added the trade with China. The Indian sub-continent presented the enterprising Liverpool merchants with raw materials as well as markets for manufactured goods. The *Kingsmill* was despatched from Liverpool by John Gladstone in 1814, and by the middle of the century India had become the next most important destination for Liverpool trade after the United States. Following the Napoleonic wars, trade was also opened up with Spanish and Portuguese colonies in Central and South America.* An accurate guide to the growth of Liverpool's maritime trade can be discerned through the total tonnage of cargo passing through the port. In 1751 it was 65,406 tons; in 1791 it had risen to 539,676 and in 1835 it stood at 1,768,426. By 1823 customs dues amounted to £1,808,402.

Although cotton was the crucially important commodity for the growth of Liverpool's power and wealth, it is important to recall also the benefits of iron during this period of time: Liverpool builders began to explore new ways of using this wonder material of the industrial age. Iron and steel were produced in Liverpool at a site in Toxteth. It opened in 1810; at its height it employed 1,500 men, but most production had ceased by the end of the nineteenth century. Although the world may rightly celebrate Abraham Darby's famous Iron Bridge at Coalbrookdale, the world has largely forgotten about the structure on the corner of Upper Parliament Street and St James Place. In 1774/75 the brick church of St James was built, a squat brick building with a square tower; it still stands, with only one claim to fame that it 'contains the earliest recorded remaining structure in cast iron in Britain.' As Quentin Hughes went on to write,

> *This in itself makes it important because cast and wrought iron were to revolutionise the architecture and engineering of the 19th century and here we see, in embryo, the start of the giant leap into vast light fireproof prefabricated structures which have transformed the appearance of Europe and America.*

---

* Trade with Spain itself had been a modest early foreign adventure for a few Liverpool merchants in the sixteenth century, although war with Spain under Elizabeth I ended this trade for some time.

St James's church, 1775, an eighteenth-century brick building that contains the earliest remaining example of structural ironwork supporting the gallery. The church has for years been out of use, but is in the care of the Redundant Churches Trust. It has recently been re-opened.

The cast-iron columns that support the gallery at St James's were predated by the iron work in St Anne's church in 1772. Liverpool led the world in this building, though sadly Liverpool also demolished it. St Anne's and St James's might not appear remarkable achievements in themselves, but they led the way to more crucially important developments along the docks and elsewhere.

The efficiency and economic success of the port depended entirely on the facilities provided by the ever-growing line of docks, which were eventually to transform nearly eight miles of Mersey shoreline. The Old Dock and the Salthouse Dock together provided only eight acres of wet dock. During the war-torn years 1756 to 1815 four new docks provided a further twenty-one acres, and over the next twenty years were constructed another eight docks and forty-five acres. Thomas Steers had been Liverpool's first dock pioneer, with his construction of the Old Dock in the first years of the eighteenth century. A century later, in 1824, Steers was followed by an even greater dock engineer, 44-year-old Yorkshireman, Jesse Hartley. Through his use of cast iron and granite, Hartley has left his indelible, beautifully crafted mark on the Mersey shore, even after the south docks lost their original use or disappeared altogether.

There were great changes ahead for the character of the vessels which were going to use the docks in the future, as announced in the *Liverpool Courier* on 5 July 1815:

> On Wednesday last, about noon, the public curiosity was considerably excited by the arrival of the first Steam Boat ever seen on our River. She came from the Clyde, and on her passage called at Ramsey in the Isle of Man, which place she left early on the same morning. We believe she is intended to ply between this port and Runcorn, or even occasionally as far as Warrington. Her cabin will contain about one hundred passengers.

Fourteen years later the *Waterloo* began service between Liverpool and Belfast, and that same year the *Savannah* arrived from America. By 1840 the Cunard steamship *Britannia* secured the transatlantic mail contract, worth £60,000, and made fifteen return crossings each year. The name of Isambard Kingdom Brunel, the greatest nineteenth-century engineer in the world, is associated with Bristol rather than Liverpool, but two of his vessels, *Great Britain* and *Great Eastern*, were both to operate out of Liverpool.

In the early days of the docks, goods had to be unloaded and transported into the town to cellars or storage rooms above workshops. Though early warehouses, usually narrow and tall, were well built, fire was an ever-present hazard. The Building Act of 1835 instructed that 'all storey posts on the ground floor shall be made of cast iron with sufficient caps and baseplates'. This recommendation was followed by the Liverpool Warehouse Act of 1843, which provided a system of registration for warehouses, which focused on fireproofing.

Under the old system goods were initially off-loaded from the ships into open low sheds along the dock side before their later removal to the warehouse. Damage and pilfering were costly, and there had been a proposal as far back as 1803 for a completely enclosed system, with warehouses surrounding the dock itself, and this gave rise in 1810 to a parliamentary bill for the construction of enclosed dockside warehouses; vested interests blocked the scheme, however, and Liverpool lost out and Thomas Telford constructed St Katherine's Dock in London as the first enclosed system in the country.

Undaunted, Jesse Hartley presented plans for a seven-acre dock surrounded by massive warehouses: the Albert Dock as it became known, was opened by Prince Albert in July 1845 and remains today as the largest Grade 1 listed building in the country. Photographs can convey the character and quality of Hartley's achievements in iron and brick far more effectively than words, although in *Seaport*, Quentin Hughes's classic work on Liverpool, there is an account of Hartley's achievements which does justice to the quality of his works.

> *The dockland scene is formed of a vast area of granite, sandstone, brick and iron. Granite walls raise the ground above the bed of the Mersey sufficient to clear the maximum tidal variation of some thirty-three feet. The masonry is everywhere on an impressive scale with finely cut chunks of granite and sandstone, all the exposed corners and edges generously curved and meticulously modelled. Along the sea wall adjoining the outer lock gates the stone floor is swept up in a gentle curve before folding over to become the vertical surface of the break-water. This gives a warning of the nearness of the edge to people walking near the locks. Road and wall surfaces are made of a combination of giant and minute stones, a gigantic crazy paving of Cyclopean masonry put together with the precision of a jig-saw.*

Medieval Liverpool had its castle, which was as nothing compared to Jesse Hartley's walls and towers and gateways of the nineteenth century. The insignificant little settlement by a muddy tidal creek on the remote shore of Lancashire had become one of the great seaports of the world. Because of difficult terrain inland, the little medieval settlement had been remote and cut off from the rest of the country, but through the ingenuity and determination of late eighteenth- and early nineteenth-century pioneers, Victorian Liverpool had developed efficient methods of communication to transport the imports and exports of an industrial hinterland with a radius of a hundred miles.

The Sankey Brook navigation, another Liverpool world first, proved so successful that the Duke of Bridgewater employed the engineer Brindley to design and dig a canal from Manchester to Liverpool. As late as 1788, seventy pack-horses set out daily from Dale Street to Manchester, transporting goods at the not inconsiderable cost of £2 a ton. When the Bridgewater Canal was opened in 1776, transport costs were slashed to just 6 shillings a ton.

Yet the commercial importance of canals was relatively short-lived. Josiah Wedgewood's pottery and William Rathbone's cotton could be transported cheaply and safely by canal, but the service was very slow. There were delays at the dockside which, at times, meant that the cotton actually took longer to get from Liverpool to Manchester than it had taken to cross the Atlantic. Other means of transport had to be explored, and that was the reason why the Liverpool corn merchant, William Sanders, made a visit to Killingworth colliery in Northumberland to examine steam locomotives at work and to meet George Stephenson and see the progress being made on the Stockton and Darlington Railway. The idea of a new and faster mode of transport appealed to the business sense of Liverpool merchants ready to invest in the project. The first parliamentary bill, in 1825, was defeated largely as a result of the opposition of the Earls of Derby and Sefton who did not relish the idea of some new-fangled invention with steam and smoke and noise going anywhere near their estates at Knowsley and Croxteth. A year later and a re-routing of the line was the signal for the project to go ahead under the direction of George Stephenson himself.

The Liverpool and Manchester Railway was destined to be the first really significant freight and passenger line in the world. The civil engineering necessary to lay a double track the thirty-one miles between the two towns was immense. The canals had overcome the problems of gradient by means of locks; the railways would conquer them by means of bridges, cuttings, embankments and tunnels. As the line approached Liverpool it was swallowed up in the Olive Mount Cutting, an excavation up to seventy feet deep, blasted and hacked through solid rock. The passenger terminus was originally at Edge Hill and only freight proceeded through the tunnels right down to the docks. The observant passenger arriving today at Lime Street Station in the heart of the city is made vividly aware of the enormous achievements of the nineteenth-century engineers.

To decide which locomotive be selected to haul the first trains, a competition was announced for 6 October 1829. The experiment ran on for a week and on the 8th Stephenson's *Rocket* performed successfully through ten runs along 1½ miles of track and to celebrate its victory a coach-load of excited, possibly petri-fied, passengers were carried along at over twenty miles an hour. A year later, on 15 September 1830, the Liverpool to Manchester Railway was opened, by a procession of seven trains watched incredulously by thousands of people along the route. The first day of the world's first public railway was marred by the world's first railway accident when, during a stop to take on more water for the engine, William Huskisson, MP for Liverpool, got out of his carriage to go to speak to the Duke of Wellington; he did not see the danger as he crossed the line and fell and his left leg was crushed under the wheels of the *Rocket*.

JESSE HARTLEY

Jesse Hartley, son of a builder and engineer, was born in Pontefract in December 1780. His father, Bernard, had become Surveyor of Bridges to the West Riding of Yorkshire, and the young Jesse followed his lead and trained initially as a stone mason. Father and son worked together on a road bridge over the River Calder at Castleford. After a spell working in Ireland he returned to England to become Bridgemaster in Salford, a post he held until he secured a new position in Liverpool six years later, in 1824. Despite having no experience in dock construction, he was appointed Deputy Surveyor of the Liverpool Docks and before the year was out he had become Civil Engineer and Superintendent of the Dock Estate, a post he would hold with the utmost distinction for 36 years, until his death at the age of 80.

Though scathing about some aspects of Hartley's aesthetic sense, fellow Victorian architect and historian Sir James Picton was firm in his praise,

> Jesse Hartley was a man of original genius, of sterling integrity, and stern independence and self-reliance ... for thirty-six years [he] guided with a despotic sway the construction of some of the mightiest works of the kind ever erected. Personally he was a man of large build and powerful frame, rough in manner, and occasionally even rude, using expletives which the angel of mercy would not like to record, sometimes capricious and tyrannical, but occasionally, where he was attached, a firm and unswerving friend. Professionally he had grand ideas and carried them into execution with strength, solidity, and skill which have never been exceeded. Granite was the material in which he delighted to work. His walls are built with rough Cyclopean masses, the face dressed, but otherwise shapeless as from the quarry, cemented together with hydraulic lime of a consistency as hard as the granite itself.

Originally these were the dock offices. The pillars and the portico are of cast iron.

AUTHOR

The Albert Dock buildings (1848) rising above the now clean water of the docks.
AUTHOR

Hartley's monumental river wall is eleven feet thick and forty feet high and in order to ensure steady supplies of his favoured granite, he persuaded the authorities to lease a quarry at Kirkmabreck in Galloway, Scotland.

The most famous of Hartley's works, however, was the Albert Dock. In this huge, enclosed dock, cargoes could be unloaded from the ships straight into the surrounding fire-proof warehouses. He installed two lifts and two cranes: the first hydraulic warehouse equipment in Liverpool – or the world.

As there was no rock near the top of the river bed to provide foundations for the massive structure, the mud and sands had to be piled with 13,729 balks of beech and elm – 48 miles of it – over an area of 7.75 acres. The walls of the dock were of granite and the warehouses themselves were of cast iron and brick. Rising from the dock walls are a series of massive Doric columns of cast iron, each fifteen feet high and twelve and a half feet in circumference. Some 23½ million bricks were used, and the five storeys of the five warehouse buildings provided an astonishing 1¼ million square feet of storage space. The roof, unseen from the dockside, was the first completely fire-proof roof in the world.

Sir James Picton admired Hartley's engineering skill but deplored his architectural taste:

The works for strength and durability are unsurpassable, but it is to be regretted that no attention whatsoever has been paid to beauty as well as strength. The enormous pile of warehouses which looms so large upon the river, and its vastness surpasses the pyramid of Cheops, is simply a hideous pile of naked brickwork.

Later generations did not agree: for Pevsner the Albert Dock has 'no parallel anywhere and are among Liverpool's most precious architectural possessions.' Quentin Hughes wrote of its 'monumental solemnity of design, stripped of the superfluous, a sound and economic solution to a problem.'

Francis Hyde in his important *Liverpool and the Mersey* (1971) summed up the Liverpool achievements of Jesse Hartley over a hundred years after his death.

> *In 1872, the total wet dock area amounted to two hundred and fifty five and a half acres with eighteen and a quarter miles of quay space. This included the docks built before 1824 and after 1860. Jesse Hartley's contribution to the total was one hundred and forty acres of wet docks and approximately ten miles of quay space. In other words, his energy and foresight had been responsible, in a short period of thirty-six years, for the provision of more than half of Liverpool's dock area.*

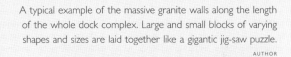

A typical example of the massive granite walls along the length of the whole dock complex. Large and small blocks of varying shapes and sizes are laid together like a gigantic jig-saw puzzle.
AUTHOR

While being a thoroughly practical man, Hartley was highly inventive and took great care over design and detailing of even the most modest of buildings.
AUTHOR

THE LIVERPOOL TO MANCHESTER RAILWAY

In 1821 a committee of twenty-three investors headed by Joseph Sanders was established to explore the feasibility of building a rail link between Liverpool and Manchester. This central group had genuine enthusiasm, but progress was slow. Eventually, the engineer George Stephenson was invited to survey the line, arriving in Liverpool on 12 June 1824. At the second attempt a bill was passed through Parliament with a healthy majority, in May 1826, and Stephenson was quickly appointed as chief engineer to the project.

The engineering problems were immense. The steep inclines presented by the sandstone ridges which form the high ground of Liverpool would prove too steep for any form of early railway, and the Olive Mount Cutting remains to this day as

This massive viaduct carries the Liverpool to Manchester line across the Sankey Valley. It remains an immensely impressive piece of civil engineering.
AUTHOR

Edge Hill Station, 1836, still operational in its original buildings.

AUTHOR

one of the deepest railway cuttings in the world – half a mile long, eighty feet deep and twenty feet wide. Where the valley of the Ditton Brook was crossed near Roby, an embankment had to be constructed over a mile in length, and fifty bridges were needed so as not to interfere with the turnpike roads along the route. One of the engineering masterpieces is the massive Sankey viaduct: nine arches sixty feet high constructed of blue brick stride majestically across the valley, offering no obstruction to the masts of the Mersey flats on the canal below, and still in use to this day. Chat Moss, an area of extremely wet peat bog, had to be traversed, and workmen had to lash planks of wood to their boots to stop themselves being sucked in. Stephenson's solution – which worked then and is still working today – was to float the rails upon great rafts of wood and heather laid upon the bog.

Stephenson knew from the start that no locomotive of his day would be able to cope with the gradients to be negotiated westwards from Edgehill into Liverpool; neither the engines nor the brakes were sufficiently powerful. Thus, the scheme was planned whereby trains would be hauled to Wapping and then later to Lime Street by stationary engines and ropes. The tunnels and cuttings through the solid rock down to Lime Street Station are awe-inspiring even in the twenty-first century.

The railway had faced fierce opposition: Lord Derby and Lord Sefton would not have the line anywhere near their country estates; canal owners saw their livelihood endangered; the frightened and the ignorant feared the worst, jeering and throwing stones. It was to take until 1836 to dig the tunnel from Crown Street to the terminus at Lime Street, but the Liverpool to Manchester Railway heralded the dawn of the Railway Age: another first for Liverpool. There had been other short stretches of railway before the Liverpool scheme, but as the world's very first public passenger and freight line, it pioneered rail transport.

THE LYCEUM POST OFFICE

The Lyceum, 1802, at the bottom of Bold Street has had a chequered history, having been designed as a gentlemen's club, thought to house the oldest proprietary circulating library in Europe.

TEN

Something to see'

A NYONE interested in knowing more about Liverpool's past must experience the same annoyance and frustration that troubled Pevsner when considering just how little pre-nineteenth-century Liverpool remains. So many of the great buildings of Liverpool appeared in the nineteenth century, sweeping aside what went before. Increasing commercial success had much to do with this process, of course, but so too did the huge population increase, which resulted in more and more people living in cramped, unpleasant and increasingly insanitary conditions.

One solution for many was to move out of the old town area. Those who could afford to move had already started, in roads such as Hanover and Duke Street, but the years between the mid-1780s and the 1840s saw very important further developments along the sandstone ridge overlooking the old town and running south from Everton in the direction of Toxteth Park. This area offered space, views down to the river and distance from the noise, squalor and smoke of the town. Before the end of the Victorian era conditions had changed dramatically, but Sir James Picton painted a very attractive picture of life in Everton fifty years earlier:

> Town and country, land and water, lay stretched beneath their view, whilst the distant sea on the one side with its ever-shifting panorama of arriving and departing vessels, and on the other, the undulating outline of the distant Welsh mountains, afforded a back-ground worthy of the scene.

Very little of a rich and elegant Everton survives today, although there are still splendid views, 250 feet above sea level, from the site of St George's church. To the south, one of Liverpool's most famous streets and indeed a whole area has survived relatively unscathed, although the functions of most of the houses have changed. Rodney Street was named to commemorate Lord Rodney's naval victory in 1780, and building work continued into the first decade of the next century. Hughes has described the street as 'Georgian urban architecture at its best', and, while the houses might have ceased to be the homes of the well-to-do, they have been preserved by the medical professions and later architects and engineers and as university administration.

In the midst of the old town dramatic changes were under way, the results of which are visible today. An Improvement Act of 1785 led the way for the widening of Castle Street, Dale Street and Water Street. At the cusp of the new century two substantial buildings were built, in 1800, which foreshadowed much that was to follow in the town centre: Heywood's Bank in Brunswick Street and the Union Newsroom in Duke Street, at one time the home of the town's first public library. The Lyceum at the bottom of Bold Street was built as a gentlemen's club which housed the oldest privately supported circulating library in Europe.

Of great civic importance was the rebuilding work on the town hall, the interior of which had been almost totally destroyed by fire in 1795 (by a great stroke of ill luck the water mains had frozen, and the flames could not be quashed). The architect James Wyatt added a portico of Corinthian columns to the front and built a circular drum to admit plenty of light and to support an impressive dome. The quality and character of the exterior stonework and the high quality of the interior features and decoration indicate just how far the town had developed since the days of John Crosse and his modest Exchange building.

There was record of only one life being lost when the town hall was gutted, but on the morning of Sunday 11 February 1810 twenty-three lives were lost when the spire and tower of St Nicholas' church collapsed. The church had undergone many additions and changes over its long history. A spire had been added in 1746, and the walls of the church rebuilt in 1774. There was instability in part of the foundations of the tower, while vibrations set up by the ringing of the bells were blamed for causing both spire and tower to collapse through the roof of the church just as the children from the Moorfields Charity School were entering the church. Following the tragedy, Liverpool's waterfront skyline was changed once again, as rebuilding work was undertaken almost immediately to the designs of Thomas Harrison of Chester. The present tower and lantern, rising 180 feet, has survived despite the almost total destruction of the main body of the church on 21 December 1940.

Four years after the building of the new church tower, the old building called the Tower, one-time residence of the Stanleys, was demolished, another important piece of Liverpool history to be lost. The fortunes of the building had fallen since the days when the earls of Derby might be in residence; it had become a cramped and squalid town gaol.

Once the draining of the area of the old Mosslake, which had once fed water into the Pool, was complete, the whole area was laid out with wide roads and elegant squares in the first part of the nineteenth century. It is now possible to walk along Percy Street, Falkner Street and Square, Canning Street, Huskisson Street, Gambier Terrace and Abercromby Square and imagine what life must have been like for the merchant princes whose fortunes depended on the docks and the workers cramped in cellars and courts down in the old town. A very forward-looking idea was introduced in 1816 to lay out 'a spacious handsome public road with wide footpaths planted on each side with two rows of trees'. The Council rejected the idea and a great opportunity was lost.

A significant open space within the area of development was the site of an extensive stone quarry, source of stone for some of the town's buildings including the town hall. The spoil heaps from the quarry on the west side of Quarry Hill were levelled and the area laid out as gardens, although a terrace of houses was built at the northern end which stood until the building of the cathedral in the twentieth century. Between 1825 and 1829, the chasm left behind by the quarry was developed as a privately funded cemetery; the mortuary chapel, which looks rather like a little Greek temple, was designed by John Foster in 1829. It still stands today as a beautiful classical building alongside the largest gothic cathedral in Britain. Meanwhile the little round classical building near the centre of the cemetery houses the remains of the MP William Huskisson, killed by *Rocket* at the opening of the Liverpool to Manchester Railway. Sadly the cemetery was 'tidied' towards the end of the twentieth century and most of the gravestones removed, but enough remain to indicate the great breadth of society of the town's inhabitants during the nineteenth century. There are elaborate memorials to the affluent, but also chilling grey slate slabs listing the names of those who had died within the walls of the orphanage. The grave of Kitty Wilkinson is a grim reminder of the cholera epidemics which swept through not just the poorer parts of the town during the 1830s. Today the airless and unsanitary cellars and courts of the poor have all been swept away by rebuilding, slum clearance and redevelopment, but they must be remembered as a significant part of the Liverpool story.

The Union News Room (*far left*) in Duke Street, 1800.

AUTHOR

Rodney Street (*below left*), the Harley Street of Liverpool, though much of the detailing of some of the Georgian windows has been lost, most of the street is well preserved and the houses, no longer residences, are well maintained.

AUTHOR

(*This page*) Well-preserved examples of late eighteenth- and early nineteenth-century Liverpool houses in what is now referred to as the 'cultural' quarter containing, as it does, two cathedrals, the Philharmonic Hall and the University.

AUTHOR

The building of St Bride's church in Percy Street began in 1830.
AUTHOR

Liverpool has always been a town and city of great contrasts, particularly between rich and poor, as Peter Aughton has remarked:

It is not until the nineteenth century that facts and figures become available which tell of the terrible conditions of the poor and underprivileged members of society. In the first decades of the century the wealthy moved out of the town centre and left it to be inhabited by the growing masses of the poor and destitute. At this time there were few places in the world where the contrast between rich and poor was as marked as in Liverpool.

The last back-to-back houses in Liverpool were almost hidden between Bold Street and Duke Street.
Total refurbishment has turned them into attractive city-centre houses.

As early as 1790, one-ninth of the total population of the town lived in cellars. Fifty years later, Herman Melville, visiting from America, was shocked by the state of so many of the population:

Old women, rather mummies, drying up with slow starving and age; young girls, incurably sick, who ought to have been in hospital; sturdy men, with the gallows in their eyes, and a whining lie in their mouths; young boys, hollow-eyed and decrepit; and puny mothers, holding up puny babies in the glare of the sun, formed the main features of the scene.

At the first census of the nineteenth century, in 1801, Liverpool's population had been about 80,000. The census returns for 1841 show a rise to 223,003, and to 376,065 in 1851. No town could cope decently with such a steep increase in such a short time. On top of this, there was a huge influx of Irish immigrants during the 1840s as a result of the Irish Potato Famine, which drove tens of thousands from their homeland in search of relief and succour. Many found their way to other towns such as Preston or Manchester, but as virtually the only point of entry Liverpool saw the greatest influx, added to a housing problem that was already severe; in 1847 it was estimated that 300,000 starving Irish landed in Liverpool. Most had dreams of wanting to cross the Atlantic to start new lives in America, but many could never raise the money for the passage. A report from the Domestic Mission recorded,

Houses of the lowest class were so crowded during this period that it was common to see every apartment of the dwelling occupied by several families, without a partition or curtain to separate them … Every tide floated in a new importation of Irish misery, and the snow was loosened from our doors by hordes of bare-footed beggars.

The council could not ignore the extent of the tragedy, of living and dying near the Mersey shore, and in 1846 they appointed Dr William Henry Duncan as the first medical officer of health in the whole country. Duncan and his committee got to work and inspected 14,085 cellars, which were home to 27,123 people, and of those cellars 5,841 had stagnant pools of water below the floors. Duncan reported that about half of the working classes of the town lived in degrading squalor in back-to-back houses in miserable narrow 'courts'. From the end of the eighteenth century, landlords had been determined to maximise their rents; many had adopted schemes which enabled them to build behind the houses which fronted onto the streets. A narrow passage between the 'front houses' opened onto a narrow court with between six and twelve houses, built 'back to back' and usually three storeys high. Photographic evidence from later in the century gives at least some idea of the wretched conditions to which the people were condemned. There was usually just one tap to serve the whole court's needs for water, two privies and no proper drainage. Dr Duncan reported on one example:

> In one court I visited the other day I found the whole place was inundated with filth, having a most intolerable stench, and found that it proceeded from two ash pits in the adjoining courts having oozed through the wall; the liquid portion of it had oozed through in consequence of the imperfection of the wall.

Quentin Hughes wrote, 'In 1864 the City Engineer probably underestimated the situation when he reported 18,500 insanitary houses and over 3,000 narrow congested courts'. It is hardly surprising that typhoid and cholera claimed so many lives.

Thus, when we go on to consider some of the great buildings which crown the success of Victorian Liverpool and which reflect the story of her enormous, unprecedented and remarkable economic development, we must never be allowed to forget some of those other features which existed in Liverpool, which under-pinned the wealth of the second city of the land: the privateer; the slave trade; the slum.

Liverpool University is now responsible for the upkeep of the large central gardens which give such a sense of elegance and space to the University houses around Abercromby Square.
AUTHOR

LIVERPOOL TOWN HALL

Liverpool has had four town halls in its 800-year history, each grander than the last. The progression from a very modest Tudor building, initially with a thatched roof, to one of the most splendid town halls in the country has a lot to say about the town's growth in wealth, power and self-esteem, although the rebuildings were often prompted by necessity: the second town hall started to collapse, while the third was gutted by fire. In Britain nineteenth-century civic pride often manifested itself in impressively grand public buildings, and Liverpool was no exception.

The first town hall was not a publicly funded building at all: it was a private donation from the Crosse family.* John Crosse was a priest at St Nicholas Shambles in London. In 1515 he gave all his property in Liverpool to the town. His money endowed a chantry in the church of St Nicholas, as well as a grammar school, and most important of all a 'new house called Our Lady's House, to keep their courts and such business as they shall think most expedient'. The building was on High Street, not far from the present town hall. The first-floor room was approached by an external staircase and used for a variety of purposes – warehouse, court-room, jail, exchange, dining hall. Although there are many references to it in the Town Books, there is no contemporary illustration. This little building was still in use in 1671.

After the Restoration in 1660, Liverpool's fortunes began to increase and the need was felt for a more imposing building. In 1673 there was reference to the second hall, 'a famous town house, placed on pillars and arches of hewn stone, and underneath it the public exchange for the merchants'. Celia Fiennes described this building as a

> very pretty Exchange stands on 8 pillars besides the corners which are each treble pillars all of stone and its raled over which is very handsome town hall; over all is a tower and cuppilow that's so high that from thence one has the whole view of the town and the country round.

It did not have a long life, because by the 1740s subsidence of the pillars had made the building unsafe and it had to be demolished.

Sir James Picton's history does not suggest that there was any great regret at the demolition of the old because the fortunes of the town were rising rapidly and civic pride was beginning to demand a much more significant building:

> The town within this period had made considerable advances in commerce, wealth, and population, and it was determined to erect a new building more suitable to the altered circumstances of the time.

No less an architect than John Wood (of Bath fame) was engaged as architect; the foundation stone was laid in 1748, and in 1755 the building was completed amid festivities that continued for a week. The building was constructed on the site of

---

* Crosse Hall Street is the only visible reminder of the family today. Their hall, of course, has long since gone.

the present town hall, and engravings from the period show a building resembling the current hall but differing in many important features both outside and inside. Not content with the original building, a number of major modifications were planned, mainly by the architect James Wyatt, and the new work was supervised by John Foster.

On 18 January 1795 a disastrous fire broke out in the west side of the hall; much of the interior of the building was gutted. Undeterred, Liverpool commissioned Wyatt to improve and rebuild. Much of the basic structure from Wood's design survived and was drawn into the new plans for what was to become one of Liverpool's greatest buildings. It is not easy to get unobstructed views of the exterior because of traffic, and unfortunately large post-war buildings at the rear of the Hall are oppressive. The interior, however, is splendid. To walk through the great public rooms is to get a real insight into the wealth and opulence of Liverpool at the beginning of the nineteenth century. The building was not intended to accommodate administrative offices; it was solely for ceremonial functions, and the elegance of the staircase prepares the visitor for the upper floor, which is devoted to reception rooms, ballrooms and dining room, superbly fitted and furnished. Joseph Sharples' words sum up the Town Hall experience admirably.

This is probably the grandest suit of civic rooms in the country, an outstanding and complete example of late Georgian decoration and a powerful demonstration of the wealth of Liverpool at the opening of the nineteenth century.

The fourth Town Hall was a modification to Wood's building by James Wyatt after the disastrous fire of 1795.

AUTHOR

115

THOMAS RICKMAN AND JOHN CRAGG

The fame and significance of Thomas Rickman and John Cragg and the two churches of Saint George on the hill at Everton and Saint Michael-in-the-Hamlet to the south side of the city are linked inextricably. Seen from a distance, the two churches do not reveal any unusual features: inside, however, they are revolutionary.

The career of Thomas Rickman was extraordinarily diverse, even in the age of the polymath. He was born in Maidenhead in 1776. His first job was as a pharmacist, with an interest in surgery, but he then worked as a clerk in the corn trade. When he moved to Liverpool in 1807 he earned his living as an accountant and out of his many spare-time interests gothic architecture came to dominate his time; he spent hours inspecting and drawing churches. Despite having no formal training in the subject, he was elected Professor of Architecture at the Liverpool Academy. Rickman's terms for the principal phases of gothic architecture – Early English, Decorated and Perpendicular – are still used today, but were first written

St George's, Everton (1814) – the first of the two Rickman and Cragg churches – really it is the lightness of the interior which is such a dramatic feature.
AUTHOR

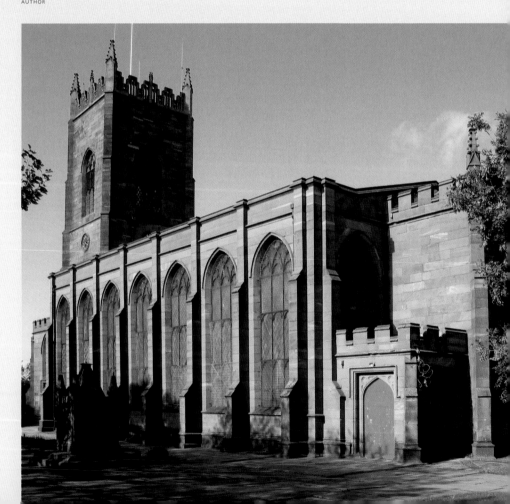

about in his *An Attempt to Discriminate the Styles of English Architecture* in 1817, a book that was very popular and became, in the words of the words of Hughes, 'the corner-stone of the Gothic revival ... The great nineteenth-century revival of Gothic was born in Rickman's researches in Liverpool ...'

Two Liverpool churches designed by Rickman survive today. Their revolutionary character was brought about after his meeting with the proprietor of the Mersey Iron Foundry, John Cragg, a tremendous enthusiast for the architectural use of cast iron, although Rickman declared 'his iron work is too stiff in his head to bend to any beauty.' Cragg had been planning to build a

St Michael-in-the-Hamlet (1815) a brick and cast-iron church built in Cragg's little 'village' and surrounded by a group of interesting houses that also employ cast iron wherever it was thought to be useful.
AUTHOR

church and had drawings prepared by architect J.M. Gandy in 1809. Cragg the iron-master and Richman the aspiring architect met in 1812, and discussions proceeded on designs for a church. A sum of £12,000 was available for the construction of a church on the site of the old beacon at Everton, and so the focus of attention moved away from Toxteth Park for a time.

The exterior of St George's, Everton, is red sandstone, which proves to be no more than a skin placed upon an internal structure of cast iron from Cragg's foundry. The results are light and airy without any of the sense of weight that can sometimes be overwhelming in a stone church. A contemporary critic was impressed in that the church showed, 'a very marked advance upon anything previously attempted in Liverpool'.

After their success in Everton, the two began work on St Michael-in-the-Hamlet, where even greater experiments were tried, in that many of the decorative features of the exterior are also of cast iron. Costs were minimised by re-using moulds, and some of the decorative elements of St George's can also be found at St Michael's. Cragg also built several houses near to the church, again making maximum use of his beloved cast iron.

In my childhood, the Mersey shore near to St Michael's was always known as the 'cast-iron shore' – the Cazzy for short. Aigburth Road is now a very busy dual carriageway, but the little 'hamlet' around the Cragg and Rickman church still retains a rather special quality. I started school there; my parents worshipped in the church towards the end of their lives; my mother's funeral was there; and Sam Kennerley, my great nephew, was brought down from his home in Cumbria to be baptised there in his grandparents' church, on 12 September 2004, followed three years later by his sister Leah.

ELEVEN

The Power and the Glory

A T T H E T I M E of Queen Victoria's coronation in 1838, Liverpool was a town of stark, sometimes brutally stark, contrasts. The majority of the population were living in wretched conditions. While trade continued to increase, the rich grew richer, and began to plan and build some of the great buildings which still remain such important features in the town. As Sally Sheard wrote in an article 'On the State of the Town of Liverpool in 1840':

> For a member of the upper classes, Liverpool in 1840 was 'the right place at the right time'. Life could be enjoyable and profitable. For the members of the lower classes it bordered on 'hell on earth', with perhaps the only consolation that it was unlikely to last more than 30 years. This 'contiguity of immense wealth and abysmal poverty' did not perhaps provoke a social conscience as it did in later decades of the century.

By 1839 the value of exports handled by the port of Liverpool was £25 million. By 1857 this figure had risen to £65 million. London had more ships than Liverpool, but Liverpool handled a greater tonnage of cargo because it could accommodate larger vessels. Although a large proportion of ordinary towns-people had to make do in courts and cellars, rich, confident and expanding Liverpool began to express her national and even international significance through great pieces of architecture. The massive growth of the docks, with their monumental warehouses, has already been mentioned, but as early as 1828 an impressive new Custom House on the site of the Old Dock made an

The Custom House, begun in 1828, was in its day one of the largest and noblest of the town's buildings. It was badly bombed during the Second World War and was not restored.

emphatic statement about the town's confidence and self-esteem. It was designed by John Foster (Senior) in a severely classical style; in its day it was the largest building in the town, costing £269,000 to build. The interior was badly damaged during the Blitz, but it was Liverpool rather than Hitler who then decided not to repair it but instead to destroy the outer walls and clear the site.

For a number of years a triennial music festival had been held in the cramped setting of St Peter's church. By 1839 the corporation felt the need for a more appropriate setting and launched a competition for a civic concert hall and followed this a year later by a competition for a design for the assize courts. Both competitions were won by the young Harvey Lonsdale Elmes, and eventually the scheme brought both plans together in the building which we now know as St George's Hall. Sadly, tuberculosis ended Elmes' life at the age of thirty-three, before his great hall was completed under the supervision first of engineer Sir Robert Rawlinson and later Professor C.R. Cockerell. The whole building was opened with a music festival in 1854. Liverpool had acquired a truly world-class building. Richard Norman Shaw declared it to be 'a building for all times, one of the great edifices of the world'. Professor Charles Reilly wrote: 'The Golden Concert Hall – one of the loveliest interiors in the world.' Pevsner wrote of it as, 'the freest neo-Grecian building in England and one of the finest in the world'. Even Queen Victoria thought it to be 'worthy of ancient Athens'.

No doubt spurred on by the imposing symbol of wealth and power of St George's Hall, a line of distinguished civic buildings arose on the north side of Shaw's Brow, soon to be renamed William Brown Street. The Library and

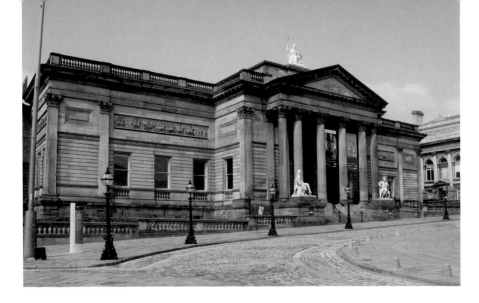

The Walker Art Gallery (1877).

AUTHOR

The Picton Reading Room (1879).

AUTHOR

Museum were built in 1860, the circular Picton Reading Room in 1879, the Walker Art Gallery in 1877 and the Sessions House in 1884. The Wellington Memorial appeared in 1863, and the Steble Fountain in front of it in 1879.

What we now know as St George's Plateau must surely always remain one of the most impressive locations in the city. Quentin Hughes is always careful in his use of words and balanced in judgement, but he has written of the area, '...

with a little imagination in design and determination in execution, this could be the finest civic parade in Britain.'

It is the sense of open space of the Plateau and William Brown Street that enables the quality of the buildings to be appreciated, and it is the lack of space down in what was the old town with its H-shaped road pattern that prevents the full appreciation of so many of the superb buildings there which had their origins in the second half of the nineteenth century.* The docks and their great attendant warehouses along the riverfront were responsible for Liverpool's increasing wealth, while the new majestic strongholds of commerce, banking and insurance wiped away the more modest houses and shops of the past. Although widened since medieval days, roads such as Water Street and Dale Street remain narrow and rarely frequented by tourists, who are often content to marvel at the architectural glories of the Pier Head. Too often when we think of tourism and great architecture, the mind goes to churches and cathedrals, stately homes, town halls and Oxbridge colleges. Would we be willing to hand over £4.50 for a conducted tour of a Victorian office block? And yet some of these buildings in the city are the work of eminent architects, and their achievements help us to understand nineteenth-century Liverpool. In the words of Quentin Hughes, 'From the 1880s onwards numerous stone palaces of business sprang up in the "down town" area, transforming domestic scale into a monumental grandeur which expresses the self-confidence of Victorian England'.

Some commercial buildings are worthy of individual notice: such as the Bank of England building (1845), The Albany (1856), Oriel Chambers (1864), Prudential Assurance (1886) and the White Star Building (1898). Peter Ellis's Oriel Chambers on Water Street, grade 1 listed, was only appreciated years after it was built as a highly original and practical piece of architecture in which glass and iron broke away from the traditional world of commercial buildings. It had not proved immediately popular among the critics: 'that large agglomeration of plate glass bubbles'. But Ellis was leading the way to producing what we now know as the modern, light-filled office block.

St George's Hall and the Plateau were the first features seen by passengers emerging from Lime Street Station which had first opened in 1836 and architect John Foster designed a dignified classical façade. This was not a Liverpool feature for long, because by 1851 the whole station was widened to cover more tracks, this time with an iron structure forming the largest single span roof anywhere in the world. In 1876 yet further widening began, Foster's façade was inadequate, and Alfred Waterhouse designed the nearby North Western Hotel.

---

* Liverpool city centre now has more listed buildings than anywhere outside London.

The excavations to carry the lines from Edge Hill through to Lime Street were immense, but as nothing when compared with the engineering skills and hard labour needed to construct a railway line actually under the Mersey. The line was opened by the Prince of Wales on 20 January 1886. Conditions in the stations and tunnels must have been dreadful, because this was before the days of electrification, but it did provide efficient commuter transport into Liverpool for people who could now choose to reside conveniently on the Wirral.

Not content with an underground railway, Liverpool built an overhead railway, in 1893, the only one in Britain, running along the line of the docks eventually from Dingle to Seaforth. For me as a child, a journey on the Overhead was exciting and intriguing, particularly when at Dingle Station passengers had to descend to the platform in a lift to board the train with its wooden carriages and loudly slamming doors. When the train eventually emerged from Dingle tunnel, the elevated line ran the full length of the docks, transporting dockers to work and people like me for a panoramic tour of the docks. It followed the line of the Dock Road and was known fondly as the dockers' umbrella.

Inside Liverpool's enclosed docks cargo could be handled efficiently between the ship and the dockside whatever the state of the tide, but passengers could not be hoisted around like bales of cotton. While the famine- and poverty-stricken Irish might tolerate uncomfortable embarkation, richer passengers sailing to and from New York would certainly not. The Cunard Company, for many years based in Liverpool, inaugurated a fortnightly sailing and the first appearance of the liner *Britannia*. In order to embark and disembark passengers whatever the height of the tide, the St George's Floating Landing Stage was opened in 1847, to be replaced in 1876 by the Prince's Stage, half a mile in length and the largest floating structure of this kind in the world and perfectly adequate to serve the vessels of the great shipping lines of the world.

Professor Ramsey Muir took stock of the growth of mercantile Liverpool as she approached the seventh centenary of the granting of the first charter; the figures were impressive. The tonnage of Liverpool shipping in 1835 was 1,768,426. By 1870 it had risen to 5,728,504 and by 1905 it was 15,996,387.

The result is, that at the end of her seventh century as a chartered borough, Liverpool finds herself amongst the three or four greatest ports of the world. She conducts one-third of the export trade, and one-fourth of the import trade, of the United Kingdom. She owns one third of the total shipping of the kingdom, and one seventh of the total registered shipping of the world. Liverpool ships are, on the average, of larger size than those of any other British port ... of every ten ships that go to and fro on all the seas of all the world, one hails from Liverpool.

The classical perfection of the Bank of England in Castle Street (1848).

The water tower at Everton (1857) – a massive piece of Victorian civil engineering that produced huge improvement to the town's water supply.

This all sounds wonderfully buoyant and healthy, yet the physical health of nineteenth-century Liverpool left much to be desired. We associate the name of Florence Nightingale with Scutari rather than Liverpool, although her influence on the nursing history of Liverpool was significant. The philanthropic work of William Rathbone has been referred to elsewhere, but his energies to improve the medical health of the people must be stressed. Through his influence developed the District Nursing Society, providing trained nurses to treat patients in their homes. On the advice of Florence Nightingale, Agnes Jones was appointed to reorganise nurses and their training at the old Workhouse Infirmary on Brownlow Hill. Liverpool's second Infirmary was proving to be inadequate, and Florence Nightingale delivered two papers on hospital design and practice in Liverpool. The third Royal Infirmary, still standing in Pembroke Place, was opened in 1888 to designs drawn by Alfred Waterhouse after consultation with Florence Nightingale.

One prominent building in Everton has an obvious connection with cleanliness and good health. The water supplied by wells at Bootle and Toxteth proved by the middle of the century to be dangerously inadequate. There were times when water was turned on for less than half an hour on alternate days and then at times of great inconvenience late at night or early in the morning. The circular Everton Waterworks were completed in 1857 to coincide with the first flow of water through the pipes all the way from the new Rivington reservoirs out in Lancashire. Demand for water increased so steadily that an even more remarkable scheme was inaugurated in 1880 whereby a valley in mid-Wales was flooded to create Lake Vyrnwy. The piping of water to Liverpool was a major civil engineering achievement.

There were some visionary minds who saw the need to preserve some green and open spaces, as lines of dreary terraced houses spread over more and more of the landscape. Liverpool has been the scene of many firsts, but not the first public park. That honour went over the water to Birkenhead when their new park, designed by Sir Joseph Paxton, was opened in 1843. Princes Park in Liverpool was planned in the same year as a private venture, although, in fact, the public did well out of it as they were given access to the whole of the central area. Around the perimeter grand houses with extensive gardens were built and the rents from these paid to support the whole park. By the end of the 1860s there were plans for Stanley, Newsham and Sefton Parks.

George's Dock in 1890. The tower of Liverpool parish church can be seen on the skyline. After the dock was filled in, the famous Pier Head buildings were constructed on the site.

Attractive and well-maintained house in Windermere Terrace, which backs on to Princes Park.

Sefton is the city's largest park and memories of it are woven into my child-hood – the boating lake, the aviary, Eros, Peter Pan, the Fairy Glen and the Iron Bridge. I can just remember walking in the Palm House before the Second World War closed it. Fortunately this vast dome of steel and glass supporting its tropical climate is functioning again, even though the city had allowed it to fall almost to ruin many years after its post-war restoration.

Families who had made fortunes on the docks or in the commercial palaces built themselves enormous houses around the fringes of the park. Most of them still exist, many in a sorry state of neglect, but they still indicate powerfully the economic success of the fortunate few. Others built smaller residential parks with gates to keep every one else out and Fulwood, Grassendale and Cressington still exist, with access to promenade walks.

In 1880 The status of Liverpool was raised by a royal charter, creating a new diocese and appointing John Charles Ryle as the first bishop, and designating Liverpool a city. In 1893 the title of Lord Mayor was conferred, and in 1895 the city boundaries were extended to include Walton, West Derby, Wavertree and Toxteth. Academic status was increased by the foundation of the new University College, housed in an ornate red-brick building at the top of Brownlow Hill.

By 1890 the British Empire covered a fifth of the land area of the globe. Between 1870 and 1900, the Empire increased by forty-five million square miles and Victoria was Queen and Empress to 400 million people – and Liverpool was the second city in the land.

ST GEORGE'S HALL

In all of the books about architecture in Liverpool architectural historians are ecstatic in their praise for St George's Hall. Unlike any other single building, it demonstrates the vitality and self-confidence of the town during a time of great economic dynamism at the start of the reign of Queen Victoria.

Yet, to me as a small boy in the 1940s, St George's Hall was menacing. In those days the Darley Dale stone was black, encrusted in soot, and the huge, cliff-like building appeared to have hardly any windows. As a teenager and student I remember being scornfully dismissive of this pseudo Graeco-Roman temple that occupied such a prominent position in the city. I frequently engaged in heated arguments with my father who was a great admirer of the building and more competent to make judgements than I was because he was at the time a Clerk of Works with Liverpool Corporation, and St George's Hall and the Town Hall were part of his brief. He had the greatest admiration for the craftsmanship of those who had built it and for the materials they had used.

Early in the nineteenth century Liverpool supported a triennial music festival and St Peter's church in Church Street was one of the principal venues. That the church should be used for the performance of oratorios displeased the Rev. Hugh McNeile and some other clergy in 1836, who protested by holding services in their own churches at the times of the concerts in an attempt to draw away the audiences. The supporters of the festival soon proposed the construction of a large building for the performance of music and other public gatherings. A subscription was opened to finance the venture and immediately raised £23,000. In 1839 there was an open competition to select an architect and a design. Seventy-five architects submitted designs, and the twenty-five-year-old Harvey Lonsdale Elmes was declared the winner.

Coincidentally, in 1835, Liverpool had become an assize town and by 1840 there was a realisation that the town needed a new and appropriate building for its new law courts, and so a second competition was advertised before any work had been started on the concert hall. Young Elmes won the second competition as well, and after a short period of proposals and counter-proposals the decision was taken to combine the two buildings, under the direction of Elmes. The great concert hall was to be at the centre with the Crown Court and Jury Room as the south end and the Civil Court and a small concert hall to the north. Although he had never visited Italy or Greece, his completed building has been described as the finest classical building in the world.

Building began in 1841 but to the concern of those who knew him Elmes' health began to deteriorate and by 1847 he was dead, having travelled to Jamaica to see whether the climate there could give him some relief. His plans were well advanced, and building continued under the supervision of the surveyor Robert Rawlinson who had worked with Elmes. Architect C.R. Cockerell was appointed architect to the project in 1851 and was responsible for most of the interior decoration and for the whole of the superb circular concert hall at the north end.

The southern end of St George's Hall. The original design was spoiled considerably when the great spread of classical sculpture had to be removed because the stonework was so badly eroded.

Below ground-floor level the public never see the massive brick arches supporting the weight of the building, nor are they aware of the Victorian ingenuity that went into the design and construction of a complex and sophisticated heating and ventilation system which washed the air and regulated the temperature according to the season and transported the treated air through a maze of ducts. Two coke boilers provided the heat source, and the air was moved by massive fans driven by steam.

The view through the main concert hall when the Minton tile mosaic floor is uncovered and light reflects from the polished red granite columns supporting the richly decorated barrel vault is staggering, grand and opulent. The small circular hall is breathtaking. Norman Shaw called it, 'a building for all times, one of the greatest edifices of the world'. Pevsner described the building as 'the freest neo-Grecian building in England and one of the finest in the world', while to Quentin Hughes it was 'a monument of world importance'.

This building reveals so much about Liverpool's story. Jesse Hartley's Albert Dock and warehouses were under construction at exactly the same time, as were the private residential parks at Fulwood, Grassendale and Cressington, Princes Park was established, and Cockerell designed the Branch Bank of England in Castle Street. What can be so easily forgotten is that this was also the age of the cholera epidemics and the first damning public health reports of Dr Duncan. Always a city of great contrast, the glory and the degradation were two faces of the same Liverpool.

DR DUNCAN

In 1846 Liverpool appointed Dr William Henry Duncan as their (and the country's) first ever medical officer of health. Liverpool, rather than being proud of their foresight, should have been deeply ashamed, because in Duncan's own words Liverpool was 'the unhealthiest town in England'. Anyone who thought about Liverpool's dramatic increase in population where there was inadequate housing, inadequate water supply and inadequate sewerage and refuse removal should have predicted the terrifying spread of disease. There was even a regulation prohibiting the connection of water closets to the sewers. The poor of Liverpool, forced to live in squalid conditions, suffered more severely than people anywhere else in the country.

By the mid-nineteenth century cholera was endemic, and there were four serious outbreaks between 1830 and 1870. The disease struck in Liverpool in April 1832, and by the end of the year 4,912 cases were reported, of whom 1,523 died. This was bad, but the results of the 1849 outbreak were even worse because 5,308 victims died in Liverpool, to be followed in 1854 by 1,290 and finally in 1866 by a further 2,122. On top of this, between June and December 1837, 524 people died of typhus and ten years later typhus accounted for one third of the town's deaths. Smallpox had not been eradicated, and 880 people died between 1837 and 1839.

Duncan was born in Scotland in 1805 and studied medicine at Edinburgh University before coming to Liverpool in 1829 and setting up his practice in Rodney Street. His public-spirited nature and concern for the poor led him also to work for the Liverpool Dispensaries and he was attached to the division in Vauxhall, the most squalid and poverty-stricken district of the town. His patients in Rodney Street could pay; the Dispensary work was supported by charity and the Church.

Three years after his establishment in Liverpool, the first cholera epidemic struck and as a result of his Rodney Street and Vauxhall Dispensary work, Duncan had a breadth of vision to enable him to comment knowledgeably on his experience of the disease. He reported in the *Liverpool Medical Gazette* in 1833 on his observations. He had treated 216 cholera cases, of whom 56 had died. There was clearly a high correlation between environment and disease. Some 97 of his patients had been living in squalid, airless conditions in courts and cellars, but only 26 in houses. One quarter of the victims forced to live in the worst conditions died. He wrote,

> ... *fever prevails at all times to a greater or lesser extent among the poor of Liverpool, and must continue to prevail so long as their inhabitations are so systematically contrived how best to accumulate filth and exclude the air of heaven.*

Duncan wrote and lectured extensively, stressing the importance of community responsibility for the health of all the members of that community.

Nothing happened quickly, but 1846 saw the publication of the Liverpool Sanitary Act and the appointment of Duncan as medical officer of health. The

The famous medical officer of health remembered today on a city centre pub sign.
AUTHOR

authorities did not see the need for a full-time appointment, and so Duncan was at first paid £500 per year for his part-time services.*

Dr Duncan's understanding of the true causes of cholera might have been erroneous, but at least he focused on environmental conditions. He worked from the idea that disease was induced by what he called 'poisonous exhalations', which arose from sewage, rubbish and general filth. His reports made public the frightful conditions under which the poor were trying to stay alive.

Possibly the most notorious district in the town was Lace Street in Vauxhall. In 1851, the street led through narrow passageways onto no fewer than 25 courts. There was a total population of 1,110. His policy of attempting to clear and put out of use the airless, damp and stinking cellars might be effective against disease, but unfortunately most of the cellar dwellers had nowhere else to go.

The courts and cellars have not survived through to today, although it was not until the 1960s that the very last of them were demolished. The remains of some back-to-back houses can be seen between Duke Street and Bold Street, but they have been almost totally rebuilt to make smart city-centre accommodation.

Duncan laboured at his post for sixteen years and died in 1863.

---

* This at the height of the Irish influx due to the Potato Famine!

LIVERPOOL'S PARKS

I was fortunate as a child to live within minutes of open spaces: the disused golf links, Otterspool Park, Jericho Lane, eventually the first section of Otterspool Promenade and, best of all, Sefton Park. My daughter has her own happy memories of time in the park with granddad, walking the dogs and feeding the ducks. Had I been born a century earlier, I would not have been so fortunate.

By the early years of the nineteenth century the town was spreading without any planning controls; people were packed into courts and mean streets and most had little chance of air and exercise in natural open spaces. As early as 1816 there was a plea to the Council for 'open pieces of land in the outskirts of the town for the amusement of the working classes', but nothing happened: local government was not yet ready to embark on such works.

In the 1840s, Richard Vaughan Yates bought some land in Liverpool and employed Paxton and James Pennethorne to design the private Princes Park, with ornamental lake, trees, grass and curving pathways around which high-quality houses for the rich would finance the upkeep of the park. An open area at Wavertree was laid out in 1856, but it was not until 1868 that Stanley, Newsham

The Palm House (1896) now restored again and in use but no longer containing quite so many exotic plants.
AUTHOR

The boating lake at Sefton Park fed by what is left of one of the ancient watercourses that eventually flowed out into the river at Otterspool.

AUTHOR

and Sefton Parks became possible through an Act of Parliament permitting the land to be purchased and planted using public money. Sefton Park was to become the largest park in the country after Regent's Park in London.

An open competition was won by Edouard Andre, a French landscape gardener, and architect Lewis Hornblower. The results of their inspiration and labour are impressive. Much of the landscape is undulating, excellent use being made of ribbon lakes to feed a large and attractive boating lake. All of the roads and pathways are curving – apart from one that did not feature in the original design. The tree planting was particularly effective, with no sense of regimented planting.

From the early 1840s some of the rich of the town built themselves spacious and attractive houses, with large gardens and forest trees in private parks running down at right angles to the river. Fulwood Park was the first though followed fairly soon by Grassendale and Cressington; the latter two had their own private riverside promenades. From 1861 onwards, Cressington had its own railway station on the Cheshire Lines, as they were called, which ran into Central Station. There was another station at Otterspool, an attractive narrow strip of parkland running from Aigburth Vale towards the river, originally the bed of the Oskelbrooke which flowed into Otters Pool, a little creek off the Mersey. In the twentieth century, the whole shore area from Beechwood Road to Jericho Lane became a municipal rubbish tip, and the made land was to become the first stretch of the Otterspool Promenade, opened in 1950.

SUDLEY HOUSE

Many of the road names around Mossley Hill were derived from the names of the houses belonging to wealthy nineteenth-century Liverpool merchants. Elmswood, Carnatic, Holmfield, Rosemont, Netherton, Barkhill, Sudley. Bark Hill House and its extensive grounds became the I. M. Marsh College of Physical Education.

And then there is Sudley House, superbly positioned in beautiful grounds which I had known from the outside as a child when my dad had an allotment on the western edge of the Sudley Estate. The house is included in Jenkins' *England's Thousand Best Houses*, in which he drew attention to the concentration of wealth in the area by the mid-nineteenth century. 'Visitors must pinch themselves to appreciate that this was once the greatest concentration of conspicuous wealth in Britain, if not in the world.'

This two-storey sandstone house in Grecian style was built about 1830. The exterior is rather plain, maybe even slightly forbidding, but it is beautifully situated almost on the top of the Mossley Hill Ridge with wonderful views to the west down to the river, across the Wirral to the hills of north Wales, and to the east over the valley and up to the wooded Woolton Ridge. The estate is protected by high sandstone walls, and there are many very fine old trees.

The Holt family were famous in Liverpool because of their shipping line. In 1884 George Holt retired, bought the house and estate, and spent the rest of his life collecting and hanging a very fine collection of paintings. He was not alone among the shipping magnates in doing this, but what is important about Sudley is that the house is very well furnished and maintained, and George Holt's pictures remain on display in the house. George's daughter, Emma, inherited the house from her father and at her death in 1944 Sudley and its contents (including works by the likes of Gainsborough, Romney, Raeburn, Reynolds, Millais, Landseer, Holman Hunt and Turner) were left to the people of Liverpool.

National Museums and Galleries on Merseyside do a remarkably good job in keeping the house and the collection safe and in good order without making it feel too like a gallery or museum. It is free from roped-off areas and restrictions. It is the perfect setting in which to wander and imagine the conditions experienced by the favoured few. Cholera might have raged in the courts of Vauxhall, but it came nowhere near here, on the breezy and leafy slopes of Mossley Hill.

Sudley House (1830s), home of the Holt family and their splendid collection of paintings. It is now part of Museums and Galleries on Merseyside.
AUTHOR

133

TWELVE

Second City

A S LIVERPOOL approached the seven hundredth anniversary of the granting of King John's charter it could justly claim to be the second city of the land, and there is ample visible evidence of the city's size and status. Boundary extensions in 1895 had brought Walton, West Derby, Wavertree and Toxteth into the city, and by 1901 the population of the new area had risen to 684,947. The geographical spread was to continue into the twentieth century, with such areas as Woolton, Childwall, and Garston, ancient settlements whose history and culture are now woven into the story of Liverpool.

Liverpool's status was acknowledged in several ways. To become a city was important and must have encouraged the citizens in some of their aspirations. Meanwhile in October 1881 a charter had been granted for the formation of a new university college which awarded degrees, validated by the Federal Victoria University. July 1903 saw the granting of the charter authorising the award of their own degrees as the University of Liverpool. The prominent Victoria Building on Brownlow Hill led to the coining of the phrase 'red-brick' university. Over 100 acres of the old Moss Lake are covered by a variety of buildings which visibly chart the first hundred years of the university's history.

The university has had many pioneering achievements. Commitment to excellence in the life sciences has featured throughout its existence, while the medical school is one of the most prestigious in the country. The university led the way with the establishment of the first department of biochemistry, the first full-time chair of dentistry, the first veterinary school, the first department of oceanography, and the first degree in social science. Eight Nobel prizewinners have spent time at Liverpool University.

View across the dock towards Pier Head. The elaborate red, striped building on the right are the former head offices of the White Star Line.

AUTHOR

The old Great North Western Hotel (1871) faces across the road to St George's Hall. After many years when the building appeared to have been abandoned, it has been converted into student accommodation.

AUTHOR

View over Salthouse dock with the brick buildings of Jesse Hartley's dock warehouses on the left and the Pier Head buildings on the right.

AUTHOR

The Victoria Building (1892), the original central building of what was to become Liverpool University. I remember sitting in tutorials in the room part-way up the tower and hearing the regular thud of the clock mechanism before it chimed the hour.

AUTHOR

Goree Piazzas in 1913. These massive warehouses on the Dock Road were destroyed in World War II.

Parallel to the birth of the university came large-scale – literally – developments for the Church of England. Until 1880 Liverpool was still part of the Diocese of Chester. With the formation of the Liverpool diocese, Bishop John Charles Ryle became its first bishop, although it was left to his successor, Francis James Chavasse, to inspire his diocese to build a great cathedral, worthy of the second city in the land. Initially, the *cathedra*, or bishop's throne, had been placed in the old St Peter's church which, despite its antiquity, was wholly unsuited to be the mother church of a diocese that stretched from Pier Head to Wigan and from north of Southport to Warrington and Widnes.

The formal decision to build a cathedral was taken at a meeting in the Town Hall in June 1901; a competition to find a suitable design was launched and, after a slightly contentious start, Giles Gilbert Scott was appointed architect in 1903. When Manchester had become a diocese in the nineteenth century, their citizens had simply adapted a medieval parish church to become the seat of the bishop. That would not do for the gentlemen of Liverpool, and when one considers the other great city buildings being built in the early years of the twentieth century it is not difficult to see why Liverpool Cathedral is as massive and splendid as it is. The foundation stone was laid the following year and building proceeded until completion in 1978. This immense gothic structure in local red sandstone, the largest cathedral in Britain, fifth largest in the world, provided what might be regarded as a time-line across the twentieth century. As a cathedral built in the age of the camera, every aspect of its construction has been recorded and it is likely to remain for a thousand years the most prominent

This 1907 view was probably taken from the tower of St Nick's and shows the Mersey Docks and Harbour board building before the Liver and Cunard buildings were started. The Overhead Railway can clearly be seen in the foreground.

feature of the local built environment. Liverpool is now famous for its two cathedrals, although building was not commenced on the Roman Catholic Cathedral for thirty years.

Civic pride was undoubtedly behind the movement for the redevelopment of the land at the Pier Head during the opening years of the twentieth century. Liverpool was one of the great seaports of the world, with a justifiably famous line of docks and warehouses, but people felt the need for some really prestigious commercial buildings that would stand out on the waterfront. As Joseph Sharples was to write, 'The Pier Head in the early twentieth century was a bustling interchange for trains, trams, ferries and ocean liners, and the buildings were conceived as landmarks, commanding attention and giving international travellers their first or last impression of the city. Seen from the water they form an unforgettable group, a symbol of maritime Liverpool at the height of its prosperity and self-confidence.' Pevsner in the generation before Sharples referred to them as representing 'great Edwardian Imperial optimism'.

The old George's Dock was drained in 1899 and the space was ready for three prestigious new buildings to express the spirit, wealth and grandeur of a great city. I never had the good fortune, literally or metaphorically, to sail into Liverpool on a Cunarder, but like thousands of others I have crossed from Woodside on a ferry boat and marvelled at the unique splendour of the Pier Head buildings, now usually refereed to as the 'three graces'. The Mersey Docks and Harbour Board Building was completed in 1907. With his usual wise insight Quentin Hughes was to write, 'Could it be that the architect intended the implication that those who worked there combined the business acumen of the Florentine bankers with the sanctity of the Church – a Renaissance merchant's palace with the dome of St Peter's perched on top?' Indeed, the dome had been designed originally by Professor Reilly as part of his plans for the cathedral. The building is as impressive inside as out, and it looks and feels like a cross between a palace and a cathedral though filled, discretely, with commerce and computers.

The Royal Liver Building in 1911 was the second of the three and it remains quite unlike any other building in the world. We have noted earlier that Liverpool has been home to some significant architectural and constructional developments, but the Liver Building was to become the most important experiment to date. When completed it was the first large-scale reinforced concrete structure in the country and one of the first in the world. Not that any of the concrete is visible to the eye, because the frame is encased in fourteen-inch thick granite. Even before its huge clock faces and copper liver birds the building was making a massive and flamboyant statement and pushing forward building techniques that would revolutionise architecture world wide.

The floating landing stage, now replaced and much enlarged.

The Cunard Steamship Company's head office was to fill the space between the first two buildings in 1914 – an Italian Renaissance palace of Portland stone supported by a concrete frame. The three buildings shout of the pride and power of a great city at the start of the twentieth century. A century later they still cannot be ignored.

Through this great city there passed thousands of rich passengers travelling in sumptuous conditions on the great Cunarders. When the *Lusitania* sailed from Liverpool on her maiden voyage in 1907 she did so as the most powerful vessel ever built, winning the coveted Blue Riband for the fastest ever crossing to New York. With her sister ship, the *Mauretania*, she held the prestigious award for over twenty years. To accommodate the first-class passengers travelling through the port, a new Adelphi Hotel was built in 1912 so that the visitors could be as lavishly pampered on shore as they had been at sea.

As we have noted earlier, there have been times during Liverpool's 800-year history when development and progress have been slow; there have been regression rather than progress; but the mighty Liverpool of the Edwardian era enjoyed the fruits of her massive wealth and looked to the future with boundless optimism.

THE PHILHARMONIC

I am well aware that the word 'philharmonic' is normally an adjective, but to many people in Liverpool the Phil has two meanings: The Royal Liverpool Philharmonic Society and the Philharmonic Hall which is the home to an orchestra, a choir and a youth orchestra. For me the hall on the corner of Hope Street carries vivid and varied memories covering a period of more than fifty years. I first entered the hall in December 1949 to sing in the school choir that was performing as part of the Liverpool Institute Speech Day. Our music master was the legendary Dr J.E. Wallace who was also chorus master at the Phil: we all thought he must be at least ninety, but he went on terrifying and inspiring singers for another twenty years. Trebles from the Institute sang with the choir and orchestra twice in 1951 as part of the Festival of Britain celebrations, and I can claim to have performed Benjamin Britten's *Spring Symphony* under the batons of Sir Malcolm Sargent and Benjamin Britten – Sargent was easier to follow. I graduated in the Phil, wearing my dad's shoes two sizes too small for me because, having bought a gown and hood, I could not afford a new pair of black shoes. I have presented prizes and spoken at a Speech Day there, and in 2003 I rose to the giddy heights of having my name on my own dressing room when I compered the Liverpool Welsh Choral Union's annual carol concert.

The Liverpool Philharmonic Society is one of those examples of a socially divided Liverpool. At the time of the first serious cholera outbreaks that scythed through the ranks of the poor and destitute, organist William Sudlow and a group of musical enthusiasts used to meet to perform choral music in St Martin's church. Their enthusiasm led to the formation of the Liverpool Philharmonic Society on 10 January 1840. This little group of amateurs was to become the fifth oldest concert-giving organisation in the world. By 1843 they had outgrown Mr Lassell's Dancing Saloon and moved their concerts to the octagonal hall of the Collegiate Institution in Shaw Street. After the purchase of a piece of land in Hope Street the foundation stone was laid for the first Liverpool Philharmonic Hall in 1846, the opening concert being presented on 27 August 1849 before a highly select audience. The rich of the town had purchased boxes and stalls for themselves and their families in perpetuity and, at one guinea, the only public seats were so expensive as to put a severe limit on the size of the audiences. As late as 1900 rigid regulations existed whereby 'only army and naval officers, ministers of religion and members of the Proprietor's families could be admitted to their boxes'.

Elitist though it was, the Philharmonic developed world-wide renown as a concert venue; Hans Richter was to call it the 'finest in Europe', and everyone praised the excellence of the acoustic. Max Bruch and Sir Charles Halle were the two most famous nineteenth-century musicians who became Principal Conductors, and between the wars in the twentieth century Sir Henry Wood and Sir Thomas Beecham led the society as it moved towards its centenary.

On the night of 5 July 1933, the hall caught fire and was totally destroyed together with music, instruments and nearly a hundred years of history. Though the hall had gone, the society did not give in and concerts continued less than half a mile away at the Central Hall in Renshaw Street until such time as a new hall could be completed. The most obvious choice of architect in Liverpool between the wars was Herbert Rowse, whose brick Art-deco building, on the site of the old, has been in constant use ever since. Its proscenium arch and cinema screen, which rise noiselessly out of the concert platform, is one of the sights of Liverpool. The society is uniquely fortunate in having its own hall, venue for rehearsal, performance and recording. Recording became a significant part of the society's programme under its new conductor, Dr Malcolm Sargent, after his appointment in 1944. Under his direction there was a famous recording of Elgar's great oratorio *The Dream of Gerontius*, the first ever recording of Britten's *Young Person's Guide to the Orchestra*, while William Walton conducted the first recording of his *Belshazzar's Feast*.

In her little book on the history of the Phil, *A Phoenix Transformed*, Margaret Lewis has stressed the massive social change among the concert goers after the war and the significance of the establishment of the monthly Industrial Concerts in 1946, 'conceived to enable the new, post-war workforce to enjoy classical music at a democratic, single low price'. Sir John Pritchard was Principal Conductor from 1955 to 1963 and was famous for his presentation of new music in the Musica Viva series. During his time the society was granted royal patronage and has since been known as the RLPS. Sir Charles Groves succeeded Pritchard and stayed in post until 1977. He was a very popular character in Liverpool and under his direction the musicians made history as the first British orchestra to perform all the Mahler symphonies. During Sir Charles's time, my friend and colleague Edmund 'Wally' Walters succeeded Dr Wallace as Chorus Master and annually Wally composed new carols for the Christmas concerts and called upon me to write words for his music.

Under Sir Charles, the orchestra and choir performed several major works in Liverpool Cathedral, and the relations between Cathedral and Phil became even stronger when Ian Tracey, Organist and Director of Music at the Cathedral, became Chorus Master at the Phil. During 1994–95, the Hall had to close for major rebuilding and refurbishment. Without a sufficiently large venue in which to perform, the society's future was in jeopardy and so they approached the Dean and Chapter of the Cathedral to see whether the Cathedral could accommodate 58 concerts between September 1994 and May 1995. As Cathedral Custos at that time I had to prove on paper that the exercise was feasible, and then in reality to help everything work so that the worship of the Cathedral was never disrupted and to ensure that the 'concert hall' was always ready for the musicians and their audiences. We believe that the season was another first for Liverpool as no other cathedral had ever attempted such a demanding exercise.

Art-deco brick-built exterior of the Philharmonic Hall in Hope Street (1939).
AUTHOR

GOODISON AND ANFIELD

Everyone who knows me will find it hilarious that I should be attempting to write anything about football. I am one of those people with two left feet and no great interest in watching other people kicking a ball around a field. But no story of Liverpool can be complete without reference to the game, and at least I can claim that I once saw Dixie Dean heading a ball – on the touchline at an amateur match long after his retirement; I also once met the great Bill Shankly at a college garden party. In Liverpool, football is followed with almost religious fervour and has been for over a hundred years and the Lancashire Football Association was formed in 1878 followed, four years later, by the Liverpool and District Football association.

From the earliest days, St Domingo's Church sported a football team, as did many other local churches, and by 1879 they became known as Everton. By their third season they carried off the league championship. A self-made businessman, John Houlding, became the club president in 1882. Under his direction the club moved to a site in Anfield Road, but serious disagreements split the club, some of whom crossed over Stanley Park and bought the site of what is now Goodison Park. Houlding was not going to be without his football, and established Liverpool Football Club at the Anfield ground. The popularity of the game was enormous. The twenty-first century is used to the idea that first-rate players in the Premier League are immensely rich: at the end of the nineteenth century the maximum weekly wage was fixed at £4.

Both clubs have been associated with some of the greatest names in British football. During the inter-war years, Dixie Dean scored 379 goals for Everton in

144

thirteen seasons and remains the only player to have scored 82 goals in one season. Billy Liddell's career at Liverpool was starting as Dixie Dean's was coming to a close.

Even with my lack of football knowledge, I could not escape knowing that for a time Liverpool was the football capital of the country, and under the leadership of Bill Shankly and Bob Paisley no other club came near to Liverpool in terms of success and popularity.

Four days after I took up the post of Education Officer at Liverpool Cathedral, ninety-five Liverpool supporters died at the Hillsborough Stadium at Sheffield. A fortnight later, I was in the Cathedral for the memorial service – probably the most emotion-charged service I have ever attended. The Cathedral was packed with chairs right back to the west doors. Ninety-five candles were lit, the names of the victims were processed with dignity to the high altar, and the solo treble voice of Martin Polglaze rose from profound silence, 'When you walk through the storm hold your head up high and don't be afraid of the dark.' I find it hard to contemplate that moment even now.

Bill Shankly.
AUTHOR

Dixie Dean.
AUTHOR

THE PIER HEAD

Childhood memory seems to insist that every trip 'into town' involved a visit to the Pier Head, not always to walk excitedly down the steep walkway onto the landing stage for a ferry trip to Birkenhead but always to climb onto a tram for the journey home. In those days the majority of the tram routes started from Pier Head. A ferry journey to Birkenhead, where they had blue buses, or better still to Seacombe or New Brighton, where they had yellow buses, was even better. Then you could stand on the upper deck and pretend you were sailing in from America to be welcomed by the three buildings that symbolised Liverpool for most travellers: The Liver building, The Cunard Building and the Mersey Docks and Harbour Board Building, the Pier Head skyline unique to Great Britain and to the world.

It is not surprising that Edwardian Liverpool, one of the richest and most powerful commercial centres of the world, should have planned to embark on such a splendid skyscape. Pevsner referred to them as 'Edwardian Imperial optimism'. The old St George's Dock had become obsolete and was to be filled in thereby producing a most prestigious building site on which Liverpool could flaunt her commercial glory. The Mersey Docks and Harbour Board Building was designed in 1900, construction commenced in 1903 and was completed in 1907. In bright sunlight on a breezy day, this elaborate baroque building shines in white Portland stone but that skin of stone encloses twentieth century building materials and techniques. The structure itself is not of stone but of steel encased in concrete and the whole faced in Portland stone. The great drum and copper-covered dome appears as the central feature of the whole design but it was an after-thought to make the building appear more impressive. Originally it had been part of Charles Reilly's unsuccessful design for Liverpool Cathedral. Internally the vistas are quite spectacular particularly in the central octagonal hall. Several writers have

The Cunard Building (1916).
AUTHOR

commented that the building seems a strange fusion of palace and church, and Sharples's words are particularly apt when he describes it as 'a secular cathedral of commerce'.

If visitors to the city are called to remember one single building that speaks to them of the city, a high proportion will name the Liver Building. It is certainly not the greatest piece of architecture but to everyone it is Liverpool. The Royal Liver Friendly Society employed architect Walter Aubrey Thomas to design their new headquarters, just over the road from his earlier Tower Building. The Liver Building is the first large reinforced concrete framed building in Britain and one of the first in the world. The grey granite blocks are simply cladding: the weight of the whole is taken by the frame. As a building site, it must have resembled a factory as raw materials were delivered onto the site, mixed in the basement and transported by electric hoist and along narrow-gauge railway tracks to where the concrete and steel were required. The speed with which this building rose might be compared with the slow progress being made at exactly the same time up on St James's Mount where the Cathedral was being built using traditional building techniques. The Cathedral took seventy four years and the Liver Building only four! The clock faces on the twin Art Nouveau towers are the largest clock faces in the world but apart from housing the mechanism, the towers have no other function than to provide perching domes for the two copper Liver Birds 295 feet above the pavement. The detailing of the building is somewhat crude, but this building is of crucial importance to the skyline of the city. It is not difficult to imagine what those towers with their Liver Birds meant to seamen on the trans-Atlantic convoys of World War Two.

The third building of the trio is the most restrained, Quentin Hughes termed it patrician alongside its plebeian granite next door neighbour. For the main offices of the Cunard Steamship Company to have been less palatial than their world-class passenger liners would have been inappropriate.

The Mersey Docks and Harbour Board Building.

AUTHOR

Pier Head memorial by William Goscombe John to the heroes of the marine engine room

THIRTEEN
Clouds over the Mersey

W H E N   T H E   P L A N S to build a great cathedral in Liverpool were proposed by Bishop Chavasse in 1901 as an old man he did not expect to see the completion of his vision, but he had no idea that it would take nearly three quarters of a century before the largest Anglican Cathedral in the world would be completed. After the laying of the foundation stone in the summer of 1904, excellent progress was made at the east end of the new building, and a large and elaborate Lady Chapel was consecrated for use on St Peter's Day 1910. There was every expectation that 1916 would see the completion of chancel and eastern transepts, but the shockwaves caused by the assassination of an archduke in a little known town in the Balkans were to have a long-term impact upon the Cathedral, the city, the nation and the world.

The Great War of 1914–18 was to make its mark on Liverpool, not in bomb sites and shattered buildings, but in a discernible slowing down in the construction of prestigious buildings. The first decade of the century saw a carry-through of late Victorian opulence in banks, commercial buildings and pubs, but the war drained confidence, costs rose and imperial self-confidence began to fade. The reasons were clear enough. The Mersey had made Liverpool a great seaport, but German submarines and torpedoes took a heavy toll on shipping and Gore's *Directory* for 1915 lists forty vessels lost, some with great loss of life. The *Lusitania* carrying 2,661 passengers and crew was attacked by a U-boat off the coast of Ireland with the loss of 1,201 lives. Two of the famous little Mersey ferry boats transported members of the Royal Marines as part of an attack on the German base at Zeebrugge: this service won the *Iris* and the *Daffodil* the prefix

Detail from the Edward Carter Preston carving on the cenotaph on St George's Plateau.
AUTHOR

Royal. Unlike the Second World War, there were no bombs along the Dock Road, but Liverpool's maritime health suffered and by the end of the war in 1918 the number of ships using the port had fallen by almost 50 per cent. Forty thousand names of servicemen who had lost their lives were eventually recorded in the memorial book to be placed on a cenotaph in the War Memorial in the Cathedral. Nearly everyone closely associated with the building of the Cathedral lost relatives, including Bishop Chavasse who lost two sons, Aidan and Noel. Noel was the only man in the Great War to be awarded the Victoria Cross and Bar for outstanding bravery, the most decorated British soldier of the conflict.

Rich, confident, flourishing Edwardian Liverpool planned and embarked upon the building of one of the greatest cathedrals in the world, but all of a sudden the power and the spirit of the Edwardian age were blasted to bits in Flanders. Where was the story of Liverpool to take her citizens next?

Unfortunately the ex-servicemen were not returning to a city 'fit for heroes'. The docks had been Liverpool's most important employer and, with fewer ships now using the port, unemployment was high. The system of employment for dockers was a disgrace. Although daily rates of pay were good, there was no certainty of employment; men had to turn up each morning hoping that they would be selected for work that day, but if they managed to secure three days of work a week they considered themselves fortunate. The Wall Street 'crash' and worldwide recession influenced the economic life of Liverpool severely, and even at the start of the Second World War the local unemployment level was still twice the national average. Liverpool had always looked to the Mersey for its prosperity: now no one was certain where future prosperity might be found.

Despite all the inter-war problems, a number of new buildings showed continuing confidence, and they say a lot about the indomitable spirit of Liverpool. India Building in Water Street was designed for the shipping company of Alfred Holt. It is a huge building occupying a whole block and right through the centre, at ground-floor level, there is a hugely impressive arcade with a painted barrel-vaulted ceiling. There are shops as well as offices and at one time it housed a bank. Its designer Herbert Rowse, who had studied architecture at the Liverpool School of Architecture, was Liverpool's most prominent architect throughout the inter-war years. Martins Bank (now Barclays) in Water Street is another Rowse masterpiece which Quentin Hughes was to describe as 'a rich, powerful, decorative building of considerable distinction and quality'. These great Rowse buildings are no denial that Liverpool faced economic and social problems, but they are evidence of a buoyant optimism.

Part of the southern end of the Queen's Drive ring road in 1908 – it was to become an extremely busy dual carriageway running in an arc around the city from north to south, from Walton to Sefton Park.

After the Philharmonic Hall in Hope Street had been destroyed by fire in 1933, it was not surprising that it was Rowse who was invited to design the city's new art-deco concert hall with excellent acoustic qualities.

Our eyes have become accustomed to black and white photographs showing some of the deplorable housing conditions so common in Liverpool during the latter years of the nineteenth century, but it remains a shock to see other photographs of deplorable housing conditions well into the twentieth century. Before the end of the First World War, 2,900 new houses and flats had been built, but conditions in the older parts of the town could still be extremely poor, with 2,770 back-to-back houses still in use. Decent houses, in what we now refer to as the suburbs, were essential to the future development of the city.

The expansion of Liverpool between the wars was dramatic and made possible by the skills of two men. John Alexander Brodie was appointed as City Engineer early in the twentieth century and Lancelot Keay was Director of Housing from 1925 and City Architect from 1938 to 1948. Brodie took up a nineteenth-century idea of building a major road around the city from Walton in the north to Aigburth in the south. Work began near Cherry Lane in 1904 and the final link through to Sefton Park was finished in 1915. As a result of the building of the great ring road, the radial routes in and out of the city such as Prescot Road and Aigburth Road were widened and Edge Lane Drive, Walton

A nostalgic view across the rooftops from Cain's Brewery towards the Cathedral. Older readers will remember the David Lewis Theatre and hostel in the centre of the shot.

This view is from the roof of the Liver Building. The long-demolished classical Custom House is in the middle distance and the chancel and eastern transepts of the Cathedral can be seen on the horizon.

Hall Avenue and Menlove Avenue were created. Without these roads, the development of the suburbs would have been impossible.

Some of the new suburban overspill developments were not without their problems, in that over-large estates in Norris Green, Huyton and Speke were completed without many necessary amenities for a contented community and were a considerable distance away from the inner-city roots of most of the inhabitants. However, Lancelot Keay designed some attractive and well-appointed little houses with areas of grass and trees. Keay was probably years ahead of his time when with he and his design team of John Hughes and Gordon Stevenson planned the St Andrew's Gardens Rehousing Scheme on one side of Brownlow Hill, just up from Lime Street Station and very close to the centre of the city. Because of its shape and design the development was nick-named the Bullring and consisted of 316 flats and plenty of recreational space. Similar flats in other parts of the city provided the early residents with the best living conditions they had ever experienced. The Bullring, refurbished and now used as student accommodation, is still in use, which is more than can be said for the soulless tower blocks of Netherley that were built fifty years later and which have already been demolished.

Speke on the south side of the city has a long and interesting history. Speke Hall, home of the Norris family since the Middle Ages, was completed by 1598 in the midst of rich farmland. The 1930s saw the development by Keay of both industrial and residential areas, but there was a serious lack of social facilities. It was near to the shores of the river and the village of Hale, there were plenty of wide roads and open spaces but serious social problems were to develop particularly after the Second World War.

Liverpool's airport was opened in Speke in 1933, and Quentin Hughes was to describe it as 'one of the first purpose-built airport terminals in the world' with a very fine terminal building that was opened in 1937. With prevailing winds from the north-west, the main take-off flight path was over one of the widest stretches of the river so controlling the noise nuisance.

Alongside the development of council estates during the inter-war years thousands of 1930s semi-detached houses were built for private ownership, and the older villages were surrounded and joined up by swathes of very decent three-bedroomed houses and reasonably sized gardens such as can be found all over the country. The nineteenth-century great houses and their estates were slowly eaten up, but living conditions were good with many wide tree-lined roads, good public transport into the city and excellent open parkland. A bold scheme for the dumping of household refuse along the shoreline at Otterspool completely covered the Mersey shore from Grassendale to the Dingle, the cast-iron shore disappeared along with the Kennerley ancestral fishermen's cottage at the bottom of Jericho Lane. The people of Liverpool would have to wait until after the Second World War before they had access to the breezy open spaces of the Otterspool Promenade.

By the inter-war years more and more people were choosing to live in the more spacious conditions in the Wirral and to travel into Liverpool each day to work. A river ferry had existed since medieval times and a railway tunnel since 1886 but road traffic still had to use the remarkable but slow Transporter Bridge at Runcorn. Work on the first Mersey road tunnel began in December 1925, and by April 1928 the pilot tunnels from Liverpool and Birkenhead met. The occasion was commemorated as Margaret Beavan, Liverpool's first Lady Lord Mayor and Alec Naylor Mayor of Birkenhead, both clad in oilskins and Wellington boots, shook hands through the small opening. The walls and the roadway were completed in 1934 together with impressive entrances ventilation shafts built to the design of Herbert Rowse. There is a family story that my mother and grandmother once walked through the tunnel – as did 299,998 other people, each paying sixpence for the privilege! At the time of its completion, the Mersey Tunnel was the longest underwater road tunnel in the world – another world first for Liverpool.

During the 1930s the massive tower of Sir Giles Scott's Anglican Cathedral was becoming a prominent feature on the Liverpool skyline. Despite world war and economic depression, the largest Anglican Cathedral in the world was well on its way towards completion. But Liverpool had a larger Roman Catholic population than any other city in the country; Liverpool was an arch-diocese, but it was an arch-diocese without a cathedral. Dr Richard Downey was appointed Archbishop in 1928 and began to investigate possible sites for a cathedral. The site of the old workhouse opposite to the University Victoria Building in Brownlow Hill was extensive and prominent and on the same ridge above the town as the emerging Anglican Cathedral. Downey made approaches to Sir Edwin Lutyens, one of the great figures of British architecture, whose enthusiastic response was immediate. It has been written that 'Lutyen's cathedral surpassed mere superlatives': the planned dome was to be a quite staggering 510 feet high, against the Anglican Cathedral's 330-feet tower, and the diameter was to be 168 feet, compared with the 137 feet of St Peter's in Rome. The foundation stone was laid in Whitsun 1933 under a tall elaborate wooden canopy that remained a prominent feature until well after the war. Five years and 2,000,000

The shot was taken in 1934 from the top of Lewis's department store looking along Renshaw Street towards St Luke's church (1831) and the partially built cathedral.

Vaulted arcade in the India Building (1923) badly damaged in the Blitz but carefully restored.

blue bricks later, the crypt was more or less complete, but by 1941 the Blitz made further building impossible and work was halted. The Lutyens design of the 1930s had as much confidence as the Edwardian Scott design along the road, but post-war austerity and realism spelled the end of such grandiose schemes. The Roman Catholic Cathedral that is now such a well-known feature of the skyline declares itself unequivocally 1960s. Lutyens' dome was just one small element of the visible destruction in the city that was brought about by the six years of the Second World War.

LIVERPOOL CATHEDRAL

By the end of the medieval period Liverpool was beginning to prove itself to be a more successful port than Chester, but Liverpool was to remain part of the Diocese of Chester until John Charles Ryle was installed as Bishop of the new Diocese of Liverpool in 1880. The old church of St Peter proved to be a wholly inadequate pro-cathedral. A contributor to the *Graphic* magazine of 1877 called it '... perhaps the ugliest and meanest building of its kind in the North of England'.

The first successful scheme to build a great new cathedral in Liverpool was launched by Bishop Francis James Chavasse in 1901. St Peter's was proving inadequate even as a temporary cathedral, and Chavasse envisaged something which would be 'a visible witness for God in the midst of the great city'. Chavasse was conscious of the gulf between the churches in Liverpool and the great secular

After Durham and Lincoln, Sir Giles Scott's Cathedral must occupy the most dramatic cathedral site in the country. At 331 feet high, the tower is visible for miles around.
AUTHOR

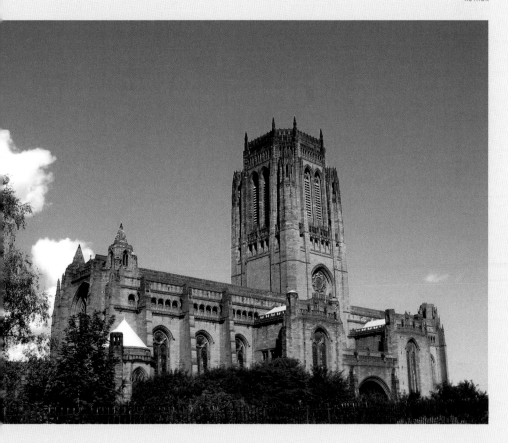

buildings. 'Why not something to speak for God in this great city as St George's Hall speaks for our great municipality?' The eventual Cathedral, in one sense a twentieth-century timeline for the whole city, has a great deal to say about the city and the community that built it. When Manchester had achieved diocesan status, the people of Manchester simply upgraded a very fine, but rather small, ancient church. Such a make-do-and-mend proposal might have satisfied the merchants of Manchester, but would not do for the gentlemen of Liverpool, who instead embarked upon the construction of what was to be the largest cathedral in Britain, the first to be built on a newly consecrated site since Salisbury in 1225, and destined to become the largest Anglican cathedral anywhere in the world. None of this is to deny that the finished cathedral is an astonishing and effective sacred space and one of the great Christian churches of the world, but the civic temple element is undeniable. The spirit and wealth and confidence that planned and built the Mersey Docks and Harbour Board Building, the Liver Building, and the Cunard building down at the Pier Head underpinned the cathedral venture too. While the Liver Building was to be one of the first large-scale reinforced concrete frame buildings in the world, Sir Giles Scott's Cathedral might well be the very last flowering of traditional Gothic. While Walter Thomas' building took four years to build, Scott's would take seventy-four.

Although there was some local disagreement, the choice of St James's Mount as the site for the new cathedral was excellent because it meant that the cathedral had such prominence, particularly when seen from the river. After considerable controversy, Giles Gilbert Scott was appointed joint architect along with Mr George Bodley. The fact that Scott was a Roman Catholic was of more significance than his young age in making his appointment highly contentious. The foundation stone was laid by King Edward VII in 1904 at a very high point in the city's prosperity and confidence. The Lady Chapel was consecrated in 1910; the high altar, chancel and eastern transepts in 1924; the central space was opened in 1941; the final finial on the tower was finished in 1942; the nave bridge was opened in 1960; and the west wall completed in 1978.

Every stage in the cathedral's development was recorded in photographs that tell a remarkable story. The project had to survive through two world wars and later a period of rocketing inflation which made its completion very difficult. In 1978 the completed building was fronted by a scene of urban decay and dereliction. It was only a stone's throw from the very centre of the Toxteth Riots. At the worst time in the 1980s when the city was in the stranglehold of the Militants, the cathedral took the initiative to develop the derelict land on its south side. Under the determined leadership of Dean Derrick Walters, the cathedral headed Project Rosemary, a development scheme to transform 45 acres of urban dereliction less than half a mile from the cathedral.

Liverpool had embarked on the building of one of the great churches of the world In the days of Edwardian opulence. As the walls of the cathedral rose, the fortunes of the city declined. It was a remarkable achievement that the cathedral, after the city's darkest days, was so important in initiating and supporting urban regeneration. A cathedral started at a time of sectarian suspicion and aggression was completed in an age of ecumenism. The cathedral that had found such difficulty in appointing a Roman Catholic architect in 1903 was the same cathedral which invited Roman Catholic Archbishop Derek Worlock to take part in the service of thanksgiving for its completion in the presence of Her Majesty Queen Elizabeth II in 1978.

Liverpool has been 'my' Cathedral for the whole of my life: I remember it with scaffolding and cranes on the tower, and I went to school in its shadow. Some people may have complained that Scott's design was a stylistic anachronism, but it is no Gothic pastiche. Its outline makes a bold statement on the skyline. The internal spaces are breath-taking. Through many years of leading parties of visitors in the building, I know that the first word used by the majority of people is 'Wow!' Although traditional in shape, with the high altar at the liturgical east end, the huge areas of floor lend themselves to considerable flexibility of layout and use. From outside, some people find the building intimidating – the tower is 331 feet high – but the warm colour of the pink sandstone helps to give the interior a welcoming atmosphere. The under-tower arches are the biggest Gothic arches ever built. At 175 feet, the tower vaulting is almost the height of Nelson's Column in Trafalgar Square. With 10,268 pipes, the Willis organ is one of the largest church organs and the bells form the highest and heaviest peal of bells anywhere in the world.

But this is Liverpool: why should anyone be surprised?

The view towards the high altar from the nave just inside the west door is breathtaking.
AUTHOR

The statue of Captain Walker at the Pier Head manages to capture the essence of indomitable Liverpool.
AUTHOR

FOURTEEN

A target of 'decisive' importance' and 'the spirit of an unconquered people'

AT THIS POINT in the storyline of the city along the Mersey shore, the nature of my knowledge changes. From King John's seven streets and a castle through centuries of town growth I have been hugely reliant on the writings of other people, but during the winter of 1939 my family brought me to live in Liverpool, I lived through the Second World War, and my mind is indelibly marked by the fragmentary but vivid personal memories of childhood experience. My reading about the war in the city Adolf Hitler declared to be a target of 'decisive importance' came years later, but I actually lived within the community in which Winston Churchill was to see 'the spirit of an unconquered people'.

Neville Chamberlain's broadcast to the nation at 11.15 a.m. on Sunday 3 September 1939 did not come as a surprise to anyone who had been reading the signs. Early that morning hundreds of anxious parents had delivered thousands of children to the stations, each child carrying a cardboard box containing a gas mask and clutching a little case or bag with a change of clothes. Children from what were considered to be danger zones were being evacuated to the country: they had no idea where they were gong and no certainty that they would ever be returned to their homes and families. There was a little note at the head of the cathedral service sheet for that morning that declared 'Because of the evacuation of the Children of the Choir the daily services in the Cathedral will be non-choral. The Congregation is asked to sing with full heart and voice all the music of the Sunday services.' Being little over a year old, I was too young for evacuation and spent all but a few 'holiday' weeks in Liverpool. I well remember some idyllic early summer days staying near Southport with my aunt, uncle and cousin, although I had no idea that while I was there Liverpool was suffering the nightly horror of the May Blitz.

The tonnage of shipping using the port in 1914 had been 19,086,672 and the 1939 figure of 21,724,050 made it clear that there had been no decline in the volume of trade; indeed it was clear that Liverpool remained in 'a position of immense strategic importance'. Liverpool was the United Kingdom's second largest port after London, handling half of the nation's imports. London and all the east-coast ports were vulnerable because of their proximity to continental Europe. Liverpool was the nation's most significant port as far as trans-Atlantic trade was concerned. The United Kingdom was importing half of its food, and the passage of raw materials and weapons through the port was also of vital importance. In 1914 the city and the nation had felt protected by the sea and their great naval forces. By 1939 it was clear that the new and greater danger came from the skies. Massive bomb destruction in Warsaw and Rotterdam gave evidence as to the power the German airforce could unleash.

The dangers to shipping were evident from the very first day when, by accident, the passenger vessel *Athenia* was torpedoed off the north-west coast of Ireland with the loss of 118 people, including many women and children. Entry into the Mersey was protected by two six-inch guns at Fort Perch Rock on the New Brighton shore and two more at Fort Crosby. An electrically activated minefield was laid between New Brighton and Gladstone dock, and torpedo tubes were installed in the floating landing stage. Human preparations involved many thousands of people, professionals and volunteers – police, fire service, salvage corps, ambulance services, rescue squads, first aid posts, air raid precautions, billeting service, fire watchers, right down, in age, to the Liverpool Civil Defence Cadet Corps – teenage boys on bicycles. I was too young to remember the preparations: all the signs of war existed and were a natural part of my life as they were for the rest of the population of Merseyside. Brick and concrete street shelters were everywhere along with Anderson shelters dug into the ground in back gardens and Morrison shelters giving service as dining tables. I do have memories of my father using timber to block in and reinforce what I came to call 'under the stairs'.

Bedtime rituals changed. Brown sticky tape had been criss-crossed over the window panes to try to prevent flying glass fragments and thick 'black-out' panels were fitted over the windows at dusk. I remember being put to bed in pyjamas and something called my 'siren suit', an all-in-one garment in blue corduroy with a zip down the front. Awake or asleep, if the siren sounded, I was lifted out of bed and placed on a little home-made camp bed under the stairs.

It was the summer of 1940 before air attacks commenced in Liverpool and part of my personal landscape was seriously damaged: Mossley Hill church is in a prominent position and although the tower remained the main body of the church sustained serious damage. By the end of September 327 people had been killed and 590 seriously injured. Five of the docks were damaged, as well as one wing of Walton Gaol and parts of Church Street and Clayton Square. Even the shelters could not guarantee safety. The night of 28/29 August saw 290 people in the shelter below a school in Durning Road when the building suffered a direct hit from a parachute mine and the structure collapsed into the shelter below. The lights fused, a boiler burst causing thick smoke, fire and flooding. The calm determination of an air-raid warden by the name of Mrs F.B. Taft meant that at least some people came out alive, but 165 people had died and 96 more were seriously injured.

After a couple of weeks of relative calm, the heaviest bombardment to date began on 20 December. There was widespread damage along the docks, and 702 people died. Among the landmarks bombed were the Dock Board Building, Cunard Building, Central Police Station, the Adelphi Hotel, the railway viaduct outside Exchange station. The old parish church of St Nicholas was gutted, while parts of St George's Hall, St John's Market, the Royal Infirmary were hit. There was also tremendous damage to shipping in the docks and in the river.

I have clear memories of the sight of the river and the city from the deck of a Mersey ferry boat. The river was full of shipping, and the Liverpool skyline was full of barrage balloons, great elephantine objects sixty-two feet long and holding 19,000 cubic feet of hydrogen. They were 'moored' at 500 feet and flown up to 5,000 feet; most of the ground bases were run by members of the Women's Auxiliary Air Force. One was stationed on the golf links at the bottom of our road, and I have memories of watching the crew trying to manage the balloon on the ground in strong wind and seeing one of the WAAFs, still clutching at the ropes, actually lifted right off her feet.

By the start of 1941, the government acknowledged the vital strategic importance of Liverpool. So much depended on the safety of the ports of Glasgow and Liverpool that Churchill was to declare 'it would seem that the problem constitutes the most dangerous part of our whole front'. Everyday life for adults in this dangerous port must have been terrifying and stressful, but for me as a little boy this was normal life. We lived within a mile of Dingle oil jetty and tank farm and a quarter of a mile from a Territorial Army barracks with search-lights and anti-aircraft guns, so the nights were often noisy. Fleets of army vehicles were parked, hidden under the trees in most of the broad pathways around Sefton Park. Our family were safe but something happened that I could not understand, although I remembered the disruption to everyday family life when we took my mother to Smithdown Road Hospital and left her there to be delivered of a still-born child.

Liverpool's early years of war were bad, but as nothing when compared with the May Blitz of 1941. In February the headquarters of Western Command had been transferred from Plymouth to the Fortress, a vast area of reinforced concrete below the Derby House wing of Exchange Buildings, directly linked to London and in total command of the vitally important safeguarding of the transatlantic convoys upon which the future of Western Europe depended. On 1 May 1941, 43 German bombers dropped 48 tons of high explosive and 112 incendiary canisters. The following night's bombardment lasted for four hours and involved 65 aircraft and caused major damage to the city centre.

Even staid and careful historians have described Saturday 3 May as 'the worst in the city's entire history'. The bombardment continued from 10.30 p.m. to 5 a.m. Not everything was to hit its target, but the Germans claimed to have dropped 363 tons of high explosive bombs and 1,380 incendiary devices. The flames from burning Liverpool were watched with horror by people over 35 miles away on the Fylde coast. The destruction adjacent to Lord Street, Paradise Street, Canning Place and south Castle Street was almost total, and the gutted site produced one of the most famous photographic images of Liverpool's war. Famous shopping centres such as Lewis's and Blackler's suffered irreparable damage. The William Brown Street buildings suffered badly; the museum was almost totally destroyed and the library lost 150,000 books. Bluecoat Chambers was gutted by fire, although the outer shell remained. Fires raged along the line of the docks and Huskisson Dock was to suffer the most devastating explosion of the war when the freighter *Malakand*, loaded with high explosives, was set on fire. Despite the most courageous efforts of a few people, the fire could not be contained and before the vessels could be scuttled the cargo began to explode. The fire took three days to burn itself out. Everything on the dock side was flattened; an anchor weighing four tons was blasted 100 yards, and some steel plates were later discovered two and a half miles away. Although fire appliances raced to help from as far afield as York, fractured water mains made their work almost impossible.

Liverpool military historian Bryan Perrett as a boy spent the night in the cellar of the family house in Edgehill and was able to record some of his vivid memories as he and his family staggered out into the morning light.

When the All Clear sounded and we emerged from the cellar and stood on the steps of the house, looking up Edge Lane towards the ridge beneath which lay the city centre. Suddenly, it all seemed very quiet. The sky was red, tinged with flickering orange. The air was acrid with the smell of burning. Fragments of ash and blackened scraps of paper were drifting down. Something heavier was smouldering in the privet hedge; it was a small square of blanket, charred around the edges.

Like many other Liverpool families, the Perretts drifted down to the city centre.

There were piles of bricks and masonry everywhere, with girders and beams protruding from them. There were tramlines twisted into impossible shapes,

The ruined shell of St Luke's church as it appeared in 2005. The tower and walls survived the bombing and have been left as a gruesome reminder of the destruction that devastated the city.
AUTHOR

All that was left of Huskisson Dock after the explosion of the Malakand.

leaning lamp standards and trailing overhead power cables. Feet crunched on billions of broken glass splinters which sparkled in the evening sunlight. Everywhere, one stepped over emergency water mains, laid above ground for the sake of speed; these sometimes crossed the road and, where they did, ramps were being constructed for motor vehicles to pass over them, although they barred the passage of trams for some time to come. At every corner familiar landmarks had vanished or been reduced to gutted shells.

Travel into and around the city on the Monday morning was almost impossible. Only 13 per cent of the tramway network was open. The Dock Road was completely blocked in eight places. Bridges over the Leeds and Liverpool Canal had been destroyed, so denying access to the north docks. Clearance work did not stop, and to prevent even further congestion only essential traffic was

Blitz destruction on Lord Street.

permitted to try to enter the central areas of the city. That night the bombers returned again, for the fifth consecutive night. Had a bomb entering the roof of the partly built Cathedral not been deflected by a massive brick wall, the damage could have been devastating. The Dean and his team of volunteer fire watchers lived in the cathedral day and night; they felt the impact of the bomb but had to wait until dawn to go outside to inspect the damage. 'It may be placed on record that the Dean, subsequently continuing his tour of the Cathedral and finding the tower had survived, tried to sing the Te Deum. In his own words – "It simply wouldn't come." Just then a blackbird somewhere in the trees outside burst into song. That was the Te Deum. The bird's liquid notes heralded the dawn.' The Cathedral had been saved, but just down the road St Luke's church had been completely gutted by incendiaries. It remains still today, a roofless monument to war, death and destruction.

A further raid on the 6th undid some of the clearance work of the previous day, and the night of the 7th, when 166 bombers dropped 232 tons of high explosives and 807 incendiaries, was even worse. The docks were paralysed, many ships severely damaged and the ferry boat *Royal Daffodil II* was sunk at Seacombe. I remember well passing aboard one of the other ferries and seeing parts of the superstructure jutting up from the muddy waters. Had the bombing continued for even a few nights longer, the port would have been out of action for months – this the judgement of Admiral Sir Percy Noble, at the time Commander Western Approaches. Even so the damage was immense in terms of buildings, shipping, docks and transport, to say nothing of the human loss. Seven nights of bombing had killed 1,453 people and left 1,065 seriously injured. But all were convinced that the indomitable spirit of Liverpool carried the day. As a military General reported, 'It is greatly to the credit of Merseyside that, in spite of an attack more severe in its weight, its concentration, and its continuity than that experienced by any other provincial centre, the port remained in action to receive the supplies that were flooding in from the United States.'

Although there were two further raids later in May and two in June, the worst of the Liverpool blitz was over. After 10 January 1942 there were no more air raids. The crucially important city on the Mersey shore had not been destroyed, but the Battle of the Atlantic raged on and the task of clearance and reconstruction must at times have appeared to be insurmountable. On 13 May 550 people had to be buried in a mass grave at Anfield Cemetery; 1,200 casualties lay seriously ill in the hospitals; 51,000 people were left homeless in the city, and another 25,000 in neighbouring Bootle. Altogether in Liverpool, Bootle, Birkenhead and Wallasey 10,000 houses had been destroyed and 184,000 damaged. For a time the Debris Clearance and Road Repair Service employed 6,000 men, whose first task was to clear and reopen 500 roads. The chaos along the docks and in the river had to be cleared – and it was.

Remarkably, building work never stopped on the cathedral, albeit with a drastically reduced workforce of elderly masons: the unfinished tower was covered in timber scaffolding lashed together with rope – a well-placed incendiary device could have been disastrous. What less propitious time could be imagined for a capping-out ceremony? Yet here, in the depths of war, with swathes of Liverpool in rubble, on a freezing cold morning in 1942, the architect, Sir Giles Scott, was photographed placing the final stone at the top of the final finial over 330 feet above floor level. When George VI visited he is reported to have said, 'Keep going whatever you do, even if you can only go on in a small way.' Prime Minister, Winston Churchill, on a visit to see damage and reconstruction said, 'I see the damage done by the enemy attacks but I also see, side by side with the devastation, and amid the ruins, quiet, confident, bright and smiling eyes, beaming with consciousness of being associated with a cause far higher and wider than any of human or personal issue. I see the spirit of an unconquerable people.'

The May Blitz was far from being the end of the war, but bombing raids after that were not so heavy and the last casualties were recorded on 10 January 1942. Though Liverpool was no longer the nightly focus of the bombing, the city was of vital importance to the war in the Atlantic to safeguard the vital convoys from America. On 7 December the Japanese attacked Pearl Harbor. America entered the war, and thousands of American troops passed through Liverpool. As Bryan Perrett wrote, 'More was to be demanded of Liverpool than at any time in its history and, because of the Luftwaffe's failure to destroy the port, Liverpool was able to respond.' Admiral Sir Max Horton became Commander in Chief Western Approaches, and the battle for survival was fought, not now over the docks and rooftops of Liverpool, but out in the North Atlantic.

In the words of the poet Dylan Thomas, 'the memories of childhood have no order and no end', and that is certainly true of my wartime memories. All that I can remember of VE Day, 8 May 1945, was being sent home from school early. At some point later was the memory of being allowed to stay up late to go out on to Aigburth Road to see the illuminated tram. Somewhere in the mists is the sight of my first banana and the vicar lighting a celebration bonfire on the golf links. I can remember powdered milk, powdered egg and long queues at the Coop, and quiet whispers about liver at the butchers, but I always seemed to have been comfortably fed. I remember the Christmas when mum's cake, after months of saving precious ingredients, was covered in marzipan because she

The laying of the foundation stone of the Metropolitan Cathedral in 1933. The wooden canopy was to remain until some years after the war when the building project was restarted to a new plan.

could not get any icing sugar, while Auntie Dodo's cake had white icing but no marzipan. Bryan Perrett's memories seem so like my own that his words make an appropriate end to this brief chapter.

> It is difficult now for the young to imagine that Liverpool was once the Second City of Empire or that the survival of the United Kingdom once depended upon the port. The incessant passage of ships on the river, the rumbling Overhead Railway, the noisy trams And the clatter of horse-drawn carts on the Dock Road have all gone, vanished into memory like the last sparks of the victory bonfires.

METROPOLITAN CATHEDRAL

I suspect that most of the Anglicans in the Diocese of Liverpool have no idea that the Roman Catholic Diocese was formed in 1850, predating the Anglican diocese by thirty years. It may well be that many Roman Catholics do not know that work on a cathedral to the design of E. W. Pugin was started in St Domingo Road, Everton, four years later but was never allowed to proceed beyond the Lady Chapel. It was left to Archbishop Richard Downey, after his appointment in 1928, to push forward plans for 'a cathedral in our time'. The choice of site was going to be important – there was already one great cathedral rising in Liverpool. The area occupied by the old workhouse at the top of the hill between Mount Pleasant and Brownlow Hill was purchased in 1930 for £100,000. Edwin Lutyens was appointed as architect, and plans were exhibited in 1932. The chosen design says much about the economic confidence of the Roman Catholic community, because this new cathedral would have dwarfed the Anglican Cathedral by a considerable margin. It was to be 680 feet in length, surmounted by a dome 168 feet in diameter and the whole building was to rise 510 feet – almost 200 feet higher than the Anglican tower. The proposed building would have accommodated 10,000 people and the estimated cost was £3 million.

Excellent progress was made on an astonishing crypt of great cavernous chapels of blue brick and granite but the Second World War interrupted operations and work stopped in 1940, Lutyens died in 1944, and it soon became obvious that with so many changed circumstances the completion of the original plans was financially impossible: the predicted cost had risen to £27 million. Adrien Scott was invited to prepare scaled-down plans but in 1959 there was an open competition for a completely new design.

Cardinal Heenan must have realised the extent of the challenge that had been placed before the architects. '... Not only by reason of its majestic beauty but because it has already cost over half a million pounds the crypt must not be abandoned ... Regard the crypt, therefore, not as an obstacle but as a challenge ... The High Altar is the central feature of every Catholic church. It must be the focus of the new building. The trend of the liturgy is to associate the congregation ever more closely with the celebrant of the Mass.' The greatest challenge of all was financial, 'Architects were simply asked to provide a building of great beauty at a small price.' This was not a condition placed before Giles Scott but he had started fifty-six years earlier in a very different Liverpool. Despite the problems, 298 architects entered the competition and the winner was Frederick Gibberd.

Gibberd's design, affectionately known as 'Paddy's Wigwam' or the 'Mersey Funnel', was revolutionary and highly successful and completed within five years at a cost of something over £1½ million. Sharples has called it 'the greatest Roman Catholic post-war architectural commission in Britain. It was also the first cathedral to break with longitudinal planning ... in favour of a centralised arrangement as encouraged by the Liturgical Movement.' The building was of its time liturgically and architecturally. The high altar, a plain block of white marble, is

in the centre of a circular building 195 feet in diameter. The celebration of the Mass is not upon some distant altar but at the very centre of the whole congregation. The great concrete and glass church with its exposed structural elements is pure 1960s. Liverpool's two cathedrals are totally different in character, but they complement each other on the city skyline. Scott's massive sandstone tower at 331 feet is balanced by the glazed lantern weighing 2,000 tons topped by a ring of steel pinnacles which give the building a height of 290 feet. Close to, the exterior may seem rather gaunt and clumsy because of the way the side chapels project – Pevsner called them 'deliberately uncouth'. They appear far more effective from inside.

The first sight of the interior can be breathtaking because of the shape and because of the power of the glass by John Piper and Patrick Reytiens. The intense blue sometimes produces in me the impression of being under the sea. I used occasionally to walk over from my workplace in the other cathedral just to spend time in a very different sacred space. Though for me the Metropolitan Cathedral lacks subtlety and is acoustically very difficult, I find it a tranquil and spiritual space. From the days of David Sheppard and Derek Worlock, the two denominations and their two cathedrals have created a strong partnership symbolised by their joint processional services between the two cathedrals at Pentecost.

Sir Frederick Gibberd's 1960s concrete cathedral – very much of its age. The interior is very striking, mainly because of the very strong coloured light from the windows.

AUTHOR

View down from the ridge at Everton in 1949. The steep slope of the hill was covered with densely packed terraced houses.

FIFTEEN

Vera Lynn to the Beatles

I SUSPECT that like many other young children of the war years, the sound of the radio was an important background to everyday life. Children's Hour was followed by the six o'clock news, and I clearly remember asking what they talked about on the news when there wasn't a war going on. Comedians Arthur Askey and Tommy Handley were nationwide favourites. Both had been born in Liverpool and had gone to school at St Michael in the Hamlet. Though decades before Top Ten and Top of the Pops, the voice of Vera Lynn singing *The White Cliffs of Dover* and *When the Lights come on again* must have haunted millions of listeners.

During the height of the Blitz, the docks and the very heart of the city had received a terrible pounding, but for the future well-being of the whole nation Liverpool had to be kept going. In the words of Francis Hyde: 'The reason for this was that London ceased to be operative for long periods, and, as a consequence, Merseyside became the most vital source of supply and despatch.' The achievement was miraculous, with over 70,000,000 tons of cargo being handled and 1,285 convoys received into the port. In fact, trade figures fluctuated considerably from year to year, and it was not until 1952 that tonnage levels reached those of 1939. The post-war years were still beset with ration books, clothing coupons, utility furniture, coal shortages and bleak, ugly bomb sites. More fundamentally, perhaps, although the earnings of the major port shipping companies were sound until the mid-1960s, it was becoming obvious in economic circles that there would have to be fundamental changes to the dock system and indeed to the whole economic foundation of the city. A series of dock strikes was a symptom of increasingly poor labour relations. The docks had been Liverpool's most significant employer; in the post-war world they would continue to be a vital feature in the city's life, but world shipping and trade were changing and Liverpool would have to change too, however painful the process.

The nineteenth century had given Liverpool its great parks, vitally important green spaces, including Sefton Park for so long a part of my childhood. There are vivid memories in summer of crowds of poorly dressed children swarming off the trams on Aigburth Road to run wild in the park and enjoy a picnic of 'jam butties' and a bottle of water. There are memories of those same children later in the day, grubby and sunburnt, sometimes with handfuls of illegally picked flowers for mum walking back up to Mill Street, Park Road and beyond because they could not persuade the 'rich' of Aigburth to 'lend' them a penny for the tram. In the summer of 1950 the first section of the Otterspool Promenade, from Mersey Road to Jericho Lane, was opened. Even the site of the long-demolished Kennerley family fishermen's hut was covered for ever, but the new public space formed a vast open, windy, riverside walkway and gardens. The city's refuse dump, covered by grass, shrubs and concrete transformed the old Mersey shore and opened up wonderful views across the river.

I had been regretting that most of my youthful memories of growing as school boy and university student in Liverpool carried little relevance for the development of the city but a couple of those memories have proved to be highly relevant. After St Michael in the Hamlet, my education continued at the Liverpool Institute High School for Boys in Mount Street and from the upper floors in that building I watched the slow post-war progress on the building of the cathedral. At last the roof went on the tower, and the highest and heaviest peal of bells anywhere in the world was installed but, for me, their presence went without notice until an event early in 1952.

On 6 February after morning break, our geography teacher, Frank Boote, came into the room and announced that King George VI was dead. The opening night of the school production of *Henry V* (with me playing the Queen of France), had to be postponed. Apart from news items and solemn music the BBC suspended normal broadcasting; and the great bourdon bell of the cathedral boomed out across the playground at the Liverpool Institute and across the rooftops of the city and the waters of the Mersey.

When I was in the sixth form I remember having some lessons with Alan Durband, one of the younger members of the English staff. He had obviously been encouraging some members of his own form, Lower 5B I think, to make imaginative use of the noticeboards in his room. A very stylish display was produced with photographs of several show-business personalities together with letters from them. The two people who were responsible for this material were

McCartney, P. and Harrison, G.: no one ever had Christian names at the Institute in those days! A few years later, while doing my postgraduate teaching certificate, I undertook my final teaching practice at Quarry Bank High School where there were still vivid memories of one Lennon, J.

It has been estimated that there were something like 300 bands playing in or near to Liverpool, but the Beatles were uniquely successful among the many well-known names who played at the Cavern, a cramped cellar in Mathew Street. *Love Me Do* hit the pop charts in 1962 and when under Brian Epstein's management they returned from their meteorically successful American tour, Liverpool went wild. I remember the difficulty I had trying to get through the centre of Liverpool on my way home that day.

On another of my teaching practices, this time at Sefton Park Secondary Modern School in a run-down, difficult area of the city, part of 'the murder mile' my tutor declared, I discovered one boy whose writing contained sparks of genuine originality. I would like to think that my teaching helped him, but I know that it did nothing of the sort. His name was Brian Patten who along with Adrien Henri and Roger McGough changed attitudes to poetry in the late 1960s through the publication of their record-breaking anthology, *The Mersey Sound*.

Liverpool, for centuries known world-wide as a sea-port, now began to be known by even more people across the world for its writers, artists and popular culture. Travellers certainly passed through the port of Liverpool in droves during the nineteenth and twentieth centuries, but Liverpool would never have

Heavy silting in an abandoned dock at low tide.
AUTHOR

called itself a tourist destination. The seeds of that change began to germinate in the 1960s and 1970s, and the Liverpool of the twenty-first century would be inconceivable without world tourism. As the south docks – the smallest in capacity and furthest from the sea – were dying, a new Liverpool was being born.

I did not see Paul McCartney after the Institute days until in the early 1990s his collaboration with conductor Carl Davies came to fruition in the cathedral in the first performance of his *Liverpool Oratorio*. I was Cathedral Custos at the time with responsibility for preparing the audience layout of the cathedral. I watched and heard all the rehearsals and both performances. I wondered what Miss Inkley, who taught Spanish to McCartney and Kennerley, would have thought had she known her Antonio Conejo stories were to reach such a vast audience. With considerable McCartney support the old Liverpool Institute building was to be transformed and extended into the Liverpool Institute of Performing Arts, and the old Speke Airport was resited, and opened as Liverpool John Lennon Airport.

As I travelled in to the university for four years I passed close to the site of the Metropolitan Cathedral, but in those years nothing seemed to be happening. Work had ceased on the Lutyens' crypt; the original scheme had to be abandoned, and the search for a new design did not begin until 1959. As Cardinal Heenan wrote later, 'We did not say whether we wanted a cathedral in a modern or a traditional style. Architects were simply asked to provide a building of great

Mathew Street was the site of the original Cavern Club, made world-famous by the Beatles.
AUTHOR

beauty at small price.' By 1967 Frederick Gibberd's concrete and glass Metropolitan Cathedral of Christ the King was completed, and the city skyline changed once more. Giles Scott's design for the Anglican Cathedral reflected the wealth and aspirations of Edwardian Liverpool and its design was part of the final flowering of gothic architecture. Though striking and memorable, the 'Met' is a smaller and more modest building and very much of its age. Cathedrals at both ends of Hope Street, respecting each other's traditions and cooperating in a variety of ways would have been inconceivable at the beginning of the twentieth century. The cooperation of the two Cathedrals is an important feature in the developing story of Liverpool.

Although the 1960s was an exciting decade in Liverpool for the economically discerning they were ominous years. A world of empire had gone, and world trade was shifting. In the final chapter of *Liverpool and the Mersey: The Development of a Port 1700–1970*, Francis Hyde's words cast serious doubt on the future:

> One cannot escape the conclusion that, in the field of labour relations, Merseyside has presented a bad image to the world … The problem of uncertainty in labour relations has been further exacerbated in recent years by changes in the cost structure of the port. Whereas, in the past, a shipping company could usually cover rising costs by an increase in receipts, the past six years have shown that this is no longer the case. In general terms, costs (mainly labour) have risen six-fold while shipping earnings have risen twofold. There has thus been a tendency for ships which have for generations used the port of Liverpool to seek out cheaper ports. In this context, continental ports, such as Rotterdam and Antwerp, have profited greatly at Liverpool's expense … The answer must lie in intensive mechanisation of the dock system. In the second place and as a corollary, the coming of container traffic must be given adequate port facilities …

The Albert Dock and its warehouses, one of the pinnacles of Jesse Hartley's mammoth Mersey shore achievements, were ahead of their day but within a generation, and long before the end of the nineteenth century, they were behind the times and unable to serve the changing trade needs of the port. For the next decade Albert Dock's future was in jeopardy and considering Liverpool's history of destroying so many of its buildings, it is a miracle that they survived at all.

POLITICIANS

I have already admitted to my lack of interest in football and footballers and all the gaps in this book are an admission of my parallel lack of interest in politics and politicians. Despite my political ignorance three politicians came to mind and I was relieved to find that the same three names featured in Arabella McIntyre-Brown's *Liverpool: The First Thousand Years*.

I have many times read the blue plaque on the wall of number 62 Rodney Street, the birthplace on 29 December 1809 of William Ewart Gladstone, the fifth of six children of John Gladstone, a very successful and public-spirited merchant. John Ewart was baptised in St Peter's church in Church Street. St Thomas's church in Seaforth and St Andrew's church in Liverpool had actually been built by John Gladstone. The fifth child of this affluent family was educated at a small school in Liverpool run by a clergyman named Rawson. William entered politics first as a Tory, but he later moved across to join the Whigs and to serve the office of Prime Minister four times between 1868 and 1894. Queen Victoria was not amused by this daunting first minister of whom she once declared, 'He speaks to me as if I were a public meeting.' Flanked by figures of Truth and Justice, W. E. Gladstone's statue stands in St John's Gardens below St George's Hall.

During Gladstone's early years of parliamentary prominence, Eleanor Frances Rathbone was born in 1872, daughter of William Rathbone VI. She was to become the most famous woman member of that remarkable Liverpool family. She had a great concern for people. She became the first woman councillor in 1909; she established the School of Social Sciences at the University. She was an Independent MP for Combined Universities from 1929 to 1945 and was the first ever woman Minister of State. She was zealous in the cause of decent housing, social reform, the position of women and the introduction of the family allowance.

A year before Eleanor Rathbone's death another remarkable Liverpool woman entered the House of Commons. In terms of background and style the two women could not have been more different, although they were both deeply committed to public service. Bessie Braddock was born in Liverpool in 1899 to very politically and socially active parents. She was taken to her first political meeting when she was only three weeks old. As a small child she helped her mother distribute food to the poor and the unemployed:

> I remember the faces of the unemployed when the soup ran out. I remember their dull eyes and their thin, blue lips. I remember blank, hopeless stares, day after day, week after week, all through the hard winter of 1906–7, when I was seven years old. I saw the unemployed all over Liverpool.

After a short period as members of the Communist Party, she and her husband John joined the Labour Party in 1926. Four years later she entered the City Council, where she held office until 1961. Between 1945 and 1970 she was MP for Liverpool Exchange Ward, and the scourge of any politician who refused to listen to her arguments. She was not popular with the establishment: 'No one takes any

Sir William Gladstone.

notice about anything unless someone does something out of order or unusual.'
You can imagine the feelings of Tory councillors when she shouted, 'I'd like to take
a machine gun to the lot of you.'

She did not court publicity for herself, and some of her causes did not draw in
popular support, but she will be remembered in her work for mental health,
prisons, and the individuals who asked for her support. She remained rooted in
Liverpool and earned the respect of thousands of people.

P O R T R A I T S

SIXTEEN

Riot and Roses

M Y HOUSE, in the green and leafy setting of the Liverpool Garden Festival, was built atop the city's rubbish tip. This afternoon I shall travel the short distance from my comfortable suburb to a little school right in the middle of Toxteth where I am Chair of Governors. If the traffic lights are in my favour, I shall be there in eight minutes, but the settings are light years apart. Poverty, unemployment, poor housing, addiction, vandalism and violence, a shifting population: all of these features are everywhere evident in the district. The Indices of Deprivation 2000 gave Granby Ward the rank order of 10 out of a total of 8,414 English wards. My next-door neighbours with their two children have just returned from a fortnight's holiday in Crete. Most of the children from my school will have to spend their summer holidays playing in the street.

The more work I do on this book, the more aware I become of the two Liverpools: what David Sheppard once called 'Enterprise City' and 'Hurt City'; from the grandeur and opulence of St George's Hall and Town Hall to the cellars and courts, from desirable Childwall to desolate Cantril Farm. Perhaps there is nothing new here: right from the time of Liverpool's industrial revolution there have been two Liverpools, of great wealth and of grinding poverty. But now, instead of poverty amid economic growth and prosperity, we were witnessing poverty and despair amid comparative and seemingly inexorable decline. Problems just below the surface could not remain submerged for ever.

Edward Patey, Liverpool's third Dean, moved up from Coventry in 1964, just two years after the Beatles first entered the charts; as he cycled to work every

In a short time, after the dock gates were left open permanently, the once-famous Albert Dock was silted up with evil-smelling mud which did nothing to help people appreciate the austere beauty of Hartley's warehouses.

day from his 'posh' suburb through the streets of Liverpool 8 he was painfully aware of some of the problems of the inner city:

> When I came to the north west from the [then] prosperous midlands, I was shocked at the state of so much of the housing. I saw terraced houses with crumbling façades, and many buildings derelict. I saw piles of rubble everywhere, slum clearance sites (I was told) waiting for redevelopment. And although here was already some relief given by new council housing estates, and housing improvement carried out by housing associations, some of these recent developments were already decaying, partly abandoned, and seriously vandalized.

In a few sentences J.F. Handley and R.W.S. Wood summed up two hundred years of local economic and social history.

> The Industrial Revolution began in Britain with north-west England, and the Mersey Basin in particular, in the forefront. Consequently, it was one of the first regions in the world to experience the full force of industrialisation and

urbanisation. The advent of a new millennium coincides with the end of that first industrial era. Indeed for the past two decades, the region has been undergoing a painful economic restructuring associated with the transition from a manufacturing to a knowledge-based economy.

The old days with the docks full of ships serviced by a huge dock workforce were over. Despite industrial developments, and industrial unrest, in the car works at Speke and other developments outside the city at Kirkby and Skelmersdale, the city seemed to be in terminal economic decline. The contrast with rich, booming industrial Manchester had never been greater as activity on the Liverpool Mersey shore slowly died. In his biography, Bishop David Sheppard succinctly crystalised the nature of the problem behind Liverpool's 'fragile' economy. 'It was a commercial city that developed around the docks, with disproportionate numbers of semi-skilled and un-skilled workers.' In 1971 unemployment in Liverpool was running at 10 per cent; by 1981 this proportion had doubled.

Three focus points in the two decades from mid-1960s to mid-1980s now emerge as of great significance in the beginnings of the slow process in the

When the Cathedral was completed in 1978, much of the setting was a drab scene of decay and urban dereliction. This photograph was taken around 1990, but today the area has been transformed.
AUTHOR

regeneration of the city: the Albert Dock, the Toxteth Riots and the International Garden Festival.

The Albert Dock had outlasted its original usefulness long before the Second World War but the German bombardment caused considerable damage, particularly to Atlantic Pavilion where serious bomb damage was simply ignored. Had it not been for the award of Grade 1 Listed status in 1952, the whole complex would probably have been swept away. Listing alone could not heal, and by 1970 everything had been cleared from the warehouses. Then the decision had been taken to close the whole of the South Docks. In September 1972 the whole system was closed. Brunswick Dock gates were opened permanently and in a remarkably short time the whole dock system was badly silted with sewage-soaked mud – over two hundred years of dock history south of Pier Head was dead.

Albert, Canning and Salthouse docks became, in the words of Joseph Sharples, 'the focus of a succession of failed, and often improbable, redevelopment proposals'. Suggestions varied from using the whole dock site for landfill to a structure 558 meters high, the tallest building in the world which would have totally obliterated everything else on the famous Pier Head skyline – and way beyond. There was government money available to bring the scattered Polytechnic buildings together in the Albert Dock, but local political wrangling led to the government's withdrawal of an offer of £3 million to help support the first phase. Central government were concerned over the seriousness of the problems. Local government changes led to the establishment of the Merseyside County Council in 1974, the body that five years later took over the South Docks. Michael Heseltine was Secretary of State for the Environment in the Thatcher government and in September 1979 he announced the government's intention of establishing the Merseyside Development Corporation which would have total control over the redevelopment of 865 acres. The Corporation came into being in March 1981.

The problems of the South Docks had rumbled on for decades, but the events on three nights in July 1981 were explosive and brought some of Liverpool's problems in banner headlines in the national press through the eruption of the Toxteth riots. The seeds of riot must have been germinating for years in poverty, poor housing, the ignoring of the problems of the indigenous black population in Granby/Toxteth and heavy-handed policing. The results of three nights of rioting in the streets around Upper Parliament street were devastation. I remember having to drive cautiously near the junction by what had once been the Rialto cinema, before it was turned into a furniture store and then gutted by fire in the riots. The main road looked like a war zone. Brixton and Toxteth were linked in people's minds through the media, and the image of Liverpool was horribly tarnished.

Life in inner-city districts such as Toxteth could indeed be grim, but some of the out-of-town overspill areas were just as bad. Cantril Farm's reputation became so blemished that after major refurbishment it had to change its name, to Stockbridge Village. By 1970 the massive rehousing scheme for 20,000 people at Netherley was established without any decent social facilities, and it soon became Liverpool's most hideous estate. Demolition was to become the only solution.

After the 1983 local elections the City Council was dominated by the Militants. Some decent council houses were built with money diverted from other areas, but there was no money for repairs for the city's ageing housing

The Albert Dock buildings might have been restored, but the 1990s still revealed swathes of land close to the city centre which appeared to have been abandoned.
AUTHOR

(*Left*) Part of the Albert Dock has been imaginatively restored as the home of the Tate.

(*Above*) The merchant vessels have gone from the South Docks, but the leisure craft have moved in and lots of new housing has transformed the area immediately south of Pier Head.

stock. The financial situation became desperate and Liverpool was once again in the headlines for all the wrong reasons. There was so much concern that serious consideration was given to putting in Government Commissioners to run the city.

The writer Beryl Bainbridge summed up Liverpool's problems by the early 1980s with real feeling.

> If I were an historian I could chart the reasons for all this chaos: the decline of trade, loss of Empire, aeroplanes instead of ships, cars instead of railways, synthetics instead of cotton, the trade unions, the rise of the Japanese. If I were a politician I could blame the Conservatives for greed, the Liberals for lack of confidence, the Socialists for naivety and jumping on the bandwagon of progress. But it hardly matters now. It's too late. Someone's murdered Liverpool and got away with it.

Vessels, temporarily or permanently to be seen near the Albert Dock are a constant reminder to visitors of Liverpool's maritime past.
AUTHOR

The murder image may sound melodramatic, but there are too many examples from the distant past as well as from the twentieth century of important communities that have shrivelled and died. But even during some of the most gloomy times Liverpool tried to look ahead so as to establish foundations for new growth. On the docks mechanisation and the rapid development of containerisation had to be the way ahead, even taking into account huge inevitable reductions of the workforce. By 1967 Gladstone Dock was operating as a container base, followed four years later by the Royal Seaforth Dock. Liverpool Freeport was launched in 1984 as the country's largest Freeport. Mersey Docks, the new body running the dock system, managed to make a profit of £800,000 in 1984, which in 2003 had risen to over £53 million. It is interesting to set these figures alongside a prediction made by Francis Hyde in his important economic history *Liverpool and the Mersey*, '... Liverpool's capacity for recovery, in times of adversity, has been that of the capacity of men and women to act in defence of their river and their port.'

A great deal of pain, frustration and destruction were unleashed by the Toxteth riots, but much new growth did follow, partly as a result of government initiative. Michael Heseltine had set up the Merseyside Development Corporation and after the riots he was designated 'Minister for Merseyside', while government money was poured in to support and attract private development, much of it along the Mersey shore. In both practical and symbolic terms the total renovation and re-launch of Albert Dock was of paramount significance. Dredging, new lock gates and bridging allowed the flow of river water back into the docks in place of the low tide depths of stinking silt. Conversion of parts of the buildings to house the prestigious Maritime Museum and Tate Liverpool were central to the whole enterprise and acted as a pump-primer for shops, restaurants, bars, exhibitions, hotels and residential accommodation.

The whole enterprise was to take years, but visible sound progress was essential for the summer of 1984 to coincide with the conclusion of the Tall Ships' Race in the Mersey and the opening of the International Garden Festival. Otterspool Promenade, city refuse dump turned open walk-way and green space, encouraged an even greater enterprise to reinstate acres of land near to the old Dingle Oil Jetty and tank farm and continue the construction of the riverside promenade – eventually all the way from Aigburth to the Pier Head. Immediately the Garden Festival was a huge success and attracted nearly three and a half million visitors. It was estimated that a million people were in the city to see the Tall Ships in just four days, and 160,000 visited Albert Dock. Indeed, the Dock was to become one of the very top free tourist attractions in the whole of the British Isles. Every time I go to Manchester, I experience a rich, powerful, productive city, in many ways more successful than Liverpool, but it can never rival Liverpool for me. In Manchester there is no Mersey Shore.

The little township of Liverpool was created in the days of King John because of the river. For half a millennium the little fishing village by the Pool seemed to be of little consequence at the far end of Lancashire until in the eighteenth and nineteenth centuries the town began to fulfil its geographical destiny by turning ever more vigorously towards the river and the economic prospects of trade with the whole world that lay beyond. The port and the docks enriched the city's vast wealth and the river, and the famous waterfront buildings were central to the tourism that was to help to revive the city in the last decades of the twentieth century. To the surprise of many people, especially those from outside the city, it was calculated that Liverpool had 2,000 listed buildings, more than any other city apart from London. To many local people the very idea of Liverpool as a centre of Heritage Tourism seemed laughable, but the redevelopment of Albert Dock and the establishment of wonderful riverside walkways began to change the whole city scene.

LIVERPOOL FREEPORT

I suspect that many of the inhabitants of Liverpool have been as ignorant as I have been about exactly what has been happening at the Port of Liverpool over the last thirty years. Everyone seems to know about the closure of the South Docks and the regeneration of the Albert Dock buildings; not so many people know anything at all about the revolution that has taken place on the Mersey shore north of the Pier Head. Much of the dockland is hidden from the motorist on the Dock Road by miles of high wall, some of brick, some of Jesse Hartley granite. I do remember driving north on the road only to find that everything had changed, I could not take my usual route because of a great sign across the road announcing Liverpool Freeport. I realised that I did not even know what a Freeport was!

Up to the mid-1960s, the port, to the outsider, must have seemed in a reasonable state of health. The 29,726,715 tons of cargo that were handled in 1966

Stacks of containers are in evidence in and around the Freeport. Containerisation has totally transformed the way in which the docks work and made the turnaround of vessels very fast.
AUTHOR

Mountains of scrap metal waiting to be loaded and exported.

was a record for the whole history of the port, but the experts recognised serious danger signs. There was a labour force of 14,000, but the systems under which the men operated were inefficient and out of line with the future of cargo handling. Casualism was still the norm. The men had to stand waiting to be invited to work, and the sessions were from 8.00 a.m. to noon and from 1 p.m. to 5 p.m. There might be some overtime from 5 to 7. There was no working on Saturday but there might be Sunday work 8 to 11 and 1 to 4. Work was slow, and a ship might be idle in dock for weeks. Though there were new practices being worked out at the new Gladstone Container Terminal, the port was in trouble. Adrian Jarvis has estimated that even in the early days of containerisation, one container vessel could transport the goods of eight conventional cargo ships. When the Mersey Docks and Harbour Board were unable to meet their debts the Mersey Docks and Harbour Company was created by Act of Parliament but Liverpool was in a mess. In the words of Philip Parker, 'The end of the 1960s and the early 1970s were years of financial crisis for the port, which came as near to closure as at any time in its history.' The

193

South Docks lacked depth for large vessels, and the quay-sides were too narrow to keep pace with changing vessels and practices; they were finally closed in 1972.

The modern Royal Seaforth Dock was opened officially in 1973, but it was obvious that major changes in working practices and manning levels would have to be confronted because continued industrial dispute and lost working days continued to ruin Liverpool's trading reputation. By 1980 there was a trading loss of £3.86 million. 1981 saw the port losing £9 million worth of trade. Fortunately decline did not last much longer. Investment in cargo-handling equipment and removal of the worst working practices began to attract trade back to the Mersey, and 1984 saw a profit of £800,000.

In the same year Liverpool Freeport was launched. This Freeport status permitted traders to hold cargo within the warehouses without having to pay VAT until the goods were sold and moved out of the Freeport. Labour problems were not over when in 1989 Mrs Thatcher and the Conservative government abolished the National Dock Labour Board scheme – no docker could be guaranteed a job for life, severance pay of £35,000 per man was available and after a seven week stoppage a reduced work-force returned to work in Liverpool, a week after everywhere else.

Records were broken in 2003 when the total freight through the port rose to 31,753,000 tonnes.

The old systems were labour-intensive, inefficient and slow. The new systems call for huge investment in machinery, a small workforce operating in shifts across a twenty-four hour period, but the result is a very fast turnround. Throughout its history Liverpool has shown itself to be at the centre of innovation, and the containerisation of dockland is just another example. Who would ever have thought of Liverpool being at the centre of a massive export trade in scrap metal, or import of coal? Or that plans were made to lengthen the landing stage so that cruise liners could be berthed at the Pier Head?

SHEPPARD AND WORLOCK

Even in my lifetime, sectarian hatred and violence in Liverpool had been powerful forces. Archbishop Beck and Bishop Stuart Blanche did much to prepare the way for what was to follow, but the importance of the joint ministries of Anglican Sheppard and Roman Catholic Worlock in the nurturing of ecumenical cooperation and in the deepest concern for the lives of the people must never be forgotten.

I suspect that many people would be hard put to name a single bishop, but during my many years working in the cathedral visitors seemed almost to expect that they might catch sight of David Sheppard. He had the good fortune, and the immense sporting skills to have been a famous cricketer and Captain of England. The whole of his ministry in the Church had been in the inner city, first in London and then for over twenty years in Liverpool. He had been Bishop of Woolwich before coming to Liverpool as its fifth bishop in 1975 and was followed a year later by Catholic Archbishop Derek Worlock who had been Bishop of Portsmouth. Temperamentally the two priests seemed totally dissimilar, but they formed a brilliant cooperative working partnership.

Sheppard's years in Liverpool are some of the most crucial years in the history of twentieth century Liverpool, years that put Liverpool on the front page of the newspapers for all the wrong reasons: industrial closures, sour labour relations, poor housing, serious local government problems, unemployment, poverty, race, riot. For these two church leaders their faith was inextricably woven into the lives of their people. They managed to win the trust of many damaged and disaffected groups and individuals and they also had access to many key political figures. During their time the relations between Roman Catholics, Anglicans and the Free Churches flourished as it had never done before in Liverpool. In their ecumenical ministry they were joined by Dr John Newton, Moderator of the Free Churches, and they were sometimes referred to as the Liverpool Three.

David Sheppard was away from Liverpool the night the Toxteth riots erupted, but he returned to the city as quickly as possible and by the third night he and Derek Worlock were out in the riot-torn streets and were instrumental in getting a megaphone for Wally Brown, the first Liverpool-born black person to be made chair of the Merseyside Community Relations Council, so that he could call upon the crowds to go home. When Lord Scarman was sent by government to examine what had happened in Toxteth, he invited Bishop and Archbishop to meet with him. The two Church leaders were strong in their support for the establishment of a law centre in Princes Road in Toxteth. Michael Heseltine as Secretary of State for the Environment was given responsibility for Liverpool, and he spent a lot of time in the city and certainly listened to what the Church leaders had to tell him.

Sheppard and Worlock faced heavy criticism from many quarters at the time, but they held firm to their convictions and were determined that the Churches should have a strong voice in the attempt to right many of the acute wrongs being suffered in the city. They were most effective in their use of the media and were held in considerable affection by a wide range of people.

SEVENTEEN
'... and hopefully revival'

I HAVE KNOWN Princes Road in Toxteth since I was a child, when I
travelled along it every day on the number 33 tram on my way to school at
the Liverpool Institute. That road is probably the best designed and most
prestigious road leading towards the city centre. It is a very wide dual carriageway
with a wide tree-lined walkway down the middle where in my youth the trams
ran. The Victorian terraces on both sides of the road are made up of very
substantial houses with well-lit spacious rooms originally inhabited by wealthy
families who were looked after by several domestic staff. The number of very
fine places of worship in such close proximity is of note: the Greek Orthodox
Church of St Nicholas (1870) stands opposite St Margaret of Antioch (1869)
designed by George Edmund Street and the Jewish Synagogue (1874). Princes
Road Presbyterian Church, Mount Zion Welsh Methodist Chapel, and Princes
Gate Baptist Chapel are long gone and Princes Road Welsh Presbyterian
Chapel gives the impression that the next winter gales might bring down even
its splendid spire. The modest new Princes Avenue Methodist Church was not
built until 1964. Though I drive along that road frequently, I had not walked
along it for years and last week I realised how much one sees travelling at four
miles an hour which you cannot hope to see driving at thirty.

Some of the houses, particularly on the east side, have been carefully restored
and maintained, but some are empty and completely derelict. Many of the
smaller streets behind the main road contain well-built late nineteenth-century
brick houses which are now empty, vandalised and boarded up. This is not the
only example of down-and-out Liverpool, but its state hits the eye so strongly

197

because less than a mile away there is a different city. I drove this morning along by the river to the parish church near to sites of massive new building. Even though it was Sunday, a demolition contractor was flattening a derelict brick building with alarming speed and a pair of cranes taller than the tower of St Nick's were both at work. There is a great sprouting of tall cranes, 42 acres of land are being redeveloped at a cost around £750,000,000. What would a visitor from outer space make of the city of Liverpool, this city of crazy contrast?

Before ideas were formalised to mark the eighth centenary of Liverpool in 2007, two extremely significant awards were made to the city. Liverpool was declared European Capital of Culture, 2008, and in 2004 UNESCO declared the city as a World Heritage Site: Liverpool – Maritime Mercantile City. After the late twentieth-century period of slow economic and social decline, the news was wonderful, and the words of Sir Neil Cossons, Chairman of English Heritage, need to be heeded in full, ' All great cities go through cycles of growth, decay, and hopefully revival.' Professor Ken Martin was well aware of the great challenge brought by the two prestigious awards: 'The ten years after the European Capital of culture in 2008 will be the ones that matter.'

My mind returns to the divided Liverpool of the past: St George's Hall and the cellars and stinking, infected courts of Vauxhall. Of course the contrast between the two Liverpools today is not nearly so marked, but the economic benefits of two prestigious international awards had to be harnessed for the general good of the whole community. Of the World Heritage Award the Duke of Westminster has said, '... this is probably one of the most exciting and important decisions to affect Liverpool since King John bestowed on it the charter of city eight centuries ago.'

Several years before the announcement of the awards, J.F. Handley and R.W.S. Wood in an academic paper had drawn attention to the place of Liverpool and its hinterland within the field of economic and social development, and their statement helps to place current developments within the whole sweep of history.

The Industrial Revolution began in Britain with north-west England, and the Mersey Basin in particular, in the forefront. Consequently, it was one of the first regions in the world to experience the full force of industrialization and urbanization. The advent of a new millennium coincides with the end of that first industrial era. Indeed, for the past two decades, the region has been undergoing a painful process of economic restructuring associated with the transition from a manufacturing to a knowledge-based economy.

There had been significant glimmers of a resurgent Liverpool even in the days of Militant domination and mis-rule. The redevelopment of the Albert Dock has already taken our attention, but another movement, less well known, can be traced up the hill to the Anglican Cathedral which at the time of its completion in 1978 was fronted by a large area of urban dereliction which caused Michael Heseltine to declare in 1981, 'A major site surrounds the magnificent Anglican Cathedral. It is a city site of world importance.' Liverpool's fourth Dean, Derrick Walters, had studied at the London School of Economics before ordination, and his zeal and entrepreneurial skills guaranteed the successful completion of the Cathedral scheme in the face of enormous problems. In order to build Dillistone and Patey Courts, originally leased to John Moores University as student accommodation, the Dean and Chapter won a £2.4 million grant and secured an additional £4.8 million from the private sector. Dean Walters was forthright in his views, 'Wealth creation and job creation are an essential part of the church's ministry. Having invested so much time and money in the building of a great cathedral, we must now be involved in the rehabilitation of the surrounding city.' Having gathered around him a skilled and specialised team, he turned his attention to 45 acres of dismal urban dereliction less than half a mile from the Cathedral. Project Rosemary headed up a regeneration scheme to cost £54 million. No other cathedral had ever led such a team, but Liverpool is used to 'firsts', and the final scheme to embrace a new Women's Hospital, a factory, university student accommodation, Housing Association and private sector housing has been a flagship for further regeneration developments.

The Dean turned his attention to zones down in the city through the creation of Rosemary Duke Street and Rosemary Chavasse. Cancer meant that Derrick Walters could not lead these schemes to a successful conclusion, but his pioneering example has been followed by others. Duke Street is being transformed, and the Grosvenor Estates scheme in the Paradise Street area must be one of the largest development schemes the city has ever seen and it cuts right across the line of flow of the old Pool. Sir David Henshaw is unequivocal in his response to the scheme. 'Here in the city we are now in a position to witness one of the largest city centre developments taking place anywhere in Europe. It is astonishing evidence of the re-emergence of Liverpool's nerve. This transformation will take people's breath away and confirm our place on the world map of dynamic cities.'

By the early 1990s, the ancient parish church of Our Lady and St Nicholas had very few residents within the parish boundaries, but by the end of the decade there had been a 300 per cent rise in population. When parishioners met

Princes Road boasts some fine houses, many, but not all, rsstored and now mainly divided into flats.

for a Think-Tank day in May 2005, the information placed before them concerning parish and Liverpool regeneration was startling. The parish population in December 2004 was 12,000, and estimated to rise to 20,000 within the next five years.

For those who had lived through Liverpool's doldrums years, there might have been justifiable scepticism at some of the rumours and news about massive construction projects in the city, but when Liverpool Vision, the City Centre Investment company published their Liverpool City Centre Development Update in February 2005, the evidence for a resurgent city was beyond doubt. The development map indicated 279 building or development projects ranging in size from £500,000 up to £750 million, many of which will be under way or completed by the time this book is published. If my arithmetic is correct, the total investment in costed projects alone approaches £2 billion. At the groundbreaking ceremony for the Paradise Street Project, Mike Storey, Leader of the City Council, said, 'This is a memorable day for Liverpool as we officially start the city's biggest-ever building project scheme of its kind in Europe. The Paradise Project will cover the equivalent of twenty-two football pitches.'

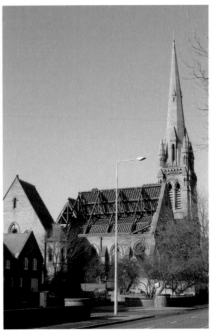

Potentially sound houses in the side streets just off Princes Road, abandoned and boarded up. Some of the newer houses in the area look dreadfully tired and neglected and are much poorer buildings than these.

AUTHOR

Princes Road, one of the finest roads into the city. Closer examination of the church reveals it to be in a dangerous state of dereliction, though since the taking of the photograph some restoration has started.

AUTHOR

The Greek Orthodox Church of St Nicholas (1870).

AUTHOR

(*Above and right*) Before and after the regeneration brought about by Project Rosemary, an urban regeneration scheme masterminded and inspired by Derrick Walters, the determined Dean of Liverpool.
AUTHOR

After years of empty office buildings, there is tremendous demand for high-grade office space at high level prices, and commercial and retail developments are being paralleled by residential new-build and imaginative conversion. For years the tawdry building right in front of Lime Street Station had been a mess and coloured rail visitors' first views of the city. Twenty five million pounds will be spent to change this. The canal age is not dead, and the Leeds and Liverpool Canal now links through to the South Docks by means of bold plans to take the waterway across the Pier Head in front of the three graces. There is a three hundred metre extension to the landing stage so that major cruise ships can once again berth in Liverpool.

Redevelopment of parts of the waterfront itself have been contentious: some mistakes have been made which have not enhanced the environment, some contentious designs have not been approved but the site of the old King's Dock, useful though it was, could not remain for ever as a car park but at last government funding has heralded the start of developments. The Deputy Prime Minister declared, 'Our cities are back and the reasons are simple. They remain the centres for wealth creation, trade and culture.'

After an uncertain start, Phil Redmond was appointed Artistic Director of the Capital of Culture Programme and made people feel confident about the whole venture. He expressed his satisfaction with the project when everything was over. He was pleased that the whole venture had added some £8 million to the Liverpool economy. An estimated 7,000 different events had been presented to a very wide public. The Tate arranged the first exhibition in Britain of the works of Gustav Klimt, and people were drawn from all over the country. At the other extreme, 125 individually decorated Lambananas brightened the streets in most unlikely places for the summer months. An exhibition of the work of architect Le Corbusier was held in the crypt of the Metropolitan Cathedral. A giant mechanical spider stalked the streets of the town centre for three days, halted the traffic and drew thousands of visitors. Sir Paul McCartney performed at Anfield and Sir Simon Rattle at the Philharmonic. No one could say that they found nothing to interest them during the year and the investment in buildings has changed the skyline.

One element of culture which is now a prominent feature in the life and economy of the city is the field of higher education. When I graduated in 1960 I suspect that the presence of a university spreading out from the Victoria Building at the top of Brownlow Hill made little impact on the community, but now between 50,000 and 60,000 students are studying for degrees at Liverpool University, John Moores University and Hope University. Architecturally, Liverpool is certainly no Oxbridge of the North West, but higher education is today a vital element in Liverpool life and the three institutions all trace their origins back into the nineteenth century.

The cholera outbreak of 1832 was the probable reason for the establishment of a Medical Institute in 1834. Before the end of the century, the city fathers saw

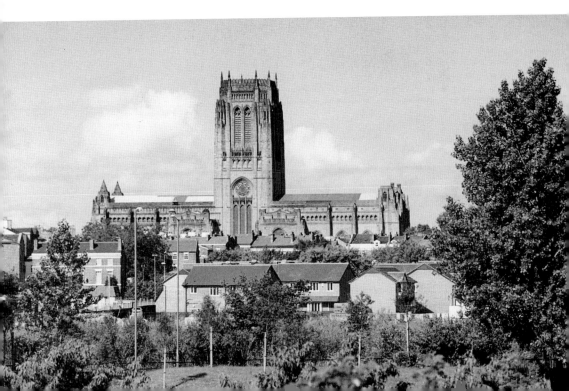

the necessity of establishing degree courses in the city, and a University College was established in 1881 to award degrees validated by the Federal Victoria University. About the time when Liverpool was feeling the need to build a great Cathedral, the city and the college achieved independent status able to validate their own degrees in 1903: a hundred years later, university buildings cover about a hundred acres of the site which was once the medieval Moss Lake.

John Moores University looks back to the Liverpool Mechanics Institute of 1825 as their origin. A number of separate higher education institutions were eventually to be drawn together as Liverpool Polytechnic on widely separated sites from Prescot and C.F. Mott College to Mossley Hill and I.M. Marsh College of Physical Education. The move towards university status was not

The Paradise Project – the whole scheme is being developed by the Duke of Westminster's Grosvenor Estates investment of £750 million. This is on the site of the Old Dock and, before that, the Pool.
AUTHOR AND GROSVENOR THE PARADISE PROJECT

without its pains but first Vice-Chancellor, Professor Peter Toyne, laboured towards the day in 1993 when Liverpool John Moores University was inaugurated at a massive ceremony in Liverpool Cathedral. An immense flame was ignited in the darkened building, wonderfully impressive, but a slightly sooty cloud floated below the vaulting for hours.

Liverpool Hope University can trace its origins in teacher education back to the days of Warrington and Notre Dame Training Colleges. Later St Katherine's, Notre Dame, and Christ's Colleges were to merge as Liverpool Institute of Higher Education. Almost miraculously in a city with a history of shameful denominational intolerance and violence, Liverpool Hope is the only fully ecumenical higher education institution in the country. It endeavours to retain a campus quality on the original green and leafy site at Childwall and later in a significant but neglected set of buildings at Everton, the site of the old St Francis Xavier's school.

The history of these three institutions has material sufficient for three individual books, but in this context all that can be done is to indicate how important higher education is in Liverpool by the first decade of the twenty-first century. Large numbers of students are now living close to the city centre. Some JMU students look out across St George's Plateau to the Hall since the university rescued the long-derelict Great North Western Hotel building which backs onto Lime Street Station. The economic benefits from three universities go well beyond the limited spending power of students. Professor Drummond Bone, Vice-Chancellor of Liverpool University declares the universities to be 'the economic drivers of their city. Guardians of civilization, the universities were also, as they are once again, the generators of innovative ideas and the generators of wealth.' Professor Michael Brown, Vice-Chancellor of JMU referred to a report prepared in the 1990s in which the city's universities were finally credited 'as a major contributing force in the economy'.

Twenty-five years ago, with the fortunes of the city in steep decline, few people would ever have thought of Liverpool as an important centre of tourism. Even ten years ago, in comic vein but never far from reality, Bill Bryson wrote about his arrival in the city: 'They were having a festival of litter when I arrived. Citizens had taken time off from their busy activities to add crisp packets, empty cigarette boxes, and carrier bags to the otherwise bland and neglected landscape.' Neglect was the characteristic feature which was most prominent to residents or visitors. You always knew when you crossed the city boundary because the roads were so in need of attention. Though declaring it to be his favourite English city, Bryson was forced to admit 'it does rather feel like a place with more past than future'. I remember showing two gentlemen from Florence around the Cathedral and up to the top of the tower. They were overwhelmed by the glories of Liverpool and asked unbelievingly, 'Where are the tourists?' They had not come from some hideous, concrete, smoke-drenched industrial town, but from a high-point of the Italian Renaissance, and they thought Liverpool was wonderful and deserved to be thronged with appreciative tourists.

Not many miles away, Chester was a very popular tourist centre particularly with American tour parties – Stratford, Chester, Lake District, Scotland. They sometimes drove through one of the tunnels glancing at Liverpool through a coach window as they headed for the M6. The occasional discerning party did come to the Cathedral, and I remember one man declaring humbly and in amazement, 'I've been in Cathedrals all over Europe, and I've never seen anything like this!'

At last, in the twenty-first century, Liverpool centre of tourism, looks to become a reality. A Centenary celebration in 2007 marked the 800th anniversary of King John's charter and regenerated interest in the city's history. The news that Liverpool had been declared European Capital of Culture for 2008 shed a search-light on the tourist potential. The World Heritage site award in 2004 was both a reward and a challenge. John Hinchcliffe is the World Heritage Officer for Liverpool City Council, a man crucial to the success of the bid and clear as to the benefits. Liverpool has achieved international acknowledgement for its significance in world history and its architectural and technological heritage. The award can help towards a much needed elevation of the whole city image and the subsequent pulling in of capital investment, grant aid and tourism. UNESCO will demand that the whole site is appropriately managed into the future and never again neglected.

During the nineteenth century those who could afford to move out from the old centre of Liverpool to fresher and leafier sites did so. By the final decade of the twentieth century there was clear evidence of a reverse trend with a population rise of 300%, up to 9,000. Imaginative conversion of large old properties into highly attractive, and expensive, apartments can be seen everywhere. A 1999 survey reported that 59% of the new residents were aged between 21 and 40, there were more men than women and 69% had university degrees. These upwardly mobile young professionals together with the new city-centre student population will change the whole character of inner-Liverpool life.

And so be it! The whole story of Liverpool has been a story of change: not of revolution but of evolution. Somehow the people of Liverpool have always managed to live through change and been enriched by change. Plague, civil war, population explosion, cellars and courts, cholera, blitz, sectarian hatred and violence, industrial unrest, riot, death of the south docks, Militant Tendency, soul-less suburbs – somehow the people of Liverpool have survived, and Liverpool can still claim greatness – not so much through the glories of its buildings, its inventions or its institutions, but through the indomitable spirit of the people of Liverpool across 800 years.

EIGHTEEN

'On the boundary'

As I contemplated writing this book, two notions were clear in my mind: I wanted to write about the visible, tangible Liverpool, the Liverpool literally on the shoreline of the Mersey, but the more I thought and struggled to find words, the more the idea of Liverpool 'on the boundary' in a more theological and philosophical way began to take hold of my thoughts. I knew that I was being drawn closer to ideas in a book I compiled and edited in 2002, *Light and Darkness, Weal and Woe: The Sermons of David Hutton*, and to one sentence in particular, 'Life and creativity lie on the boundary between order and chaos.'

As I prepared the final version of my text, the notion of a boundary seemed to embrace more and more, right from the misty medieval days to the media spotlights of the twenty-first century. King John's little settlement was established right on the western edge of a very remote region but that shore-line boundary enabled the township to develop into the supremely important north-west port. The tidal estuary itself has been on a boundary: the scouring tides at the river mouth ensured that the river remained navigable but the gently sloping shore at low tide made the loading and unloading of cargo and passenger very difficult and demanded that human ingenuity and civil engineering modify the boundary line through miles of river-wall, dock and floating landing stage.

During the years of the Victorian heyday of the docks, the port was the most important boundary point between Western Europe and the Americas. Had that boundary point failed in the Second World War, the future sovereignty of

Views of the city from the Wheel of Liverpool.
JIM CRAIG

the whole nation would have been in doubt. The post-war years put the port and its docks on another potentially fatal boundary between the old, slow, labour intensive dock system and the highly mechanised and hugely more efficient container port. In the nineteenth century the opening of the Albert Dock was a boundary point in the history of cargo handling. In the twenty-first century the re-birth of the Albert Dock as a crucial feature in the development of tourism was once again on a boundary line.

Historically Liverpool seems frequently on a tightrope between success and failure. For the first four hundred years, the town could not look to any secure and prosperous future. The very buildings of the nineteenth century reflected the unsure balance between order and chaos: the classical, prestigious glories of St George's Hall and the degrading nightmare of the airless and stinking cellars and courts. The shameful sectarian violence and bigotry of the past has established a respectful ecumenical balance even within my life time.

As the city approached the 800th anniversary of King John's Charter there was still an alarming boundary between what David Sheppard called 'Enterprise City' and 'Hurt City'. World Heritage Site, Capital of Culture and Grosvenor millions are wonderful, but areas of decay, neglect and urban desolation cannot be hidden. What can Capital of Culture and World Heritage Site do for the children in my school in Toxteth, too many of whom are 'damaged' even before they enter the education system? Near to the ancient church of Our Lady and St Nicholas are new highly prestigious apartment blocks, stylish city centre homes for a young, rich upwardly mobile population. When I walked through the churchyard on Palm Sunday morning 2005, there was someone sleeping rough in the church doorway. The remains of a couple of cardboard boxes had been placed mattress-like on the stone step, and a human figure lay shrouded in a thin sleeping bag. That boundary between order and chaos, and life and creativity in Liverpool is stark and painful.

Maybe it is because the dark-side, the negative, the chaos has been ever-present in the lives of the people of Liverpool that their life and their creativity have been such powerful forces. From the degradation of the slave ships came

Building the Leeds and Liverpool Canal link.
JIM CRAIG

A cruise ship at Liverpool

JIM CRAIG

Liverpool celebrates the 2005 Champions' League
win over A.C. Milan in Istanbul.

COURTESY OF LIVERPOOL CITY COUNCIL

213

the voices of Rathbone and Roscoe; from the disease, filth and stench of the cellars and courts came Kitty Wilkinson and Dr Duncan; from the sectarian battlegrounds Canon Major Lester and Monsignior Nugent and Sheppard and Worlock; from the squalid, ignored and poverty-stricken the unignorable Josephine Butler, Eleanor Rathbone and Bessie Braddock.

Although this little history has concentrated on the visual landscape, dock, canal, railway, great buildings and slums, everywhere behind all the buildings and construction, manipulating the landscape there are people. My reading has been awash with the names of the great: musicians, poets, artists, engineers, philanthropists, entertainers, ministers of religion, merchant princes, scholars, doctors and surgeons, architects, footballers, town-planners – the list is endless. For whatever reasons, the life and creativity of so many of the people of Liverpool have contributed to this vibrant community.

Whatever happened to the little girl who was asked in school to paint a picture of a horse? Unable to cope with this task, she painted a line of green grass. 'Where's the horse?' asked the teacher. 'It's gone for a walk,' declared the little girl without the slightest hesitation.

'Can you put me off at the Rialto?' said the large lady as she clambered on to a 33 tram in Renshaw Steet. 'No, love. I 'aven't the strength,' retorted the conductor.

In a not very good secondary modern school in the early 1960s, a rota of fourth-year boys brewed the staff tea at break time. An amiable scally, holding on to the handle, offered the Deputy Head a mug of steaming tea. 'Ow! That's hot!' said the teacher. 'So would you be if you'd just been boiled!' came the instant reply.

It might be comforting to report on a Liverpool populated only by public-spirited, warm-hearted, friendly folk, but that report would be blatantly false and takes no account of an unprovoked attack on a man by a small gang of teenagers who left him bleeding on the pavement and unconscious in hospital for over a week; the assault on an elderly pensioner in her own house; the theft of the money from the collection plate in the parish church; over thirty windows smashed for no reason at all in a school which has served its community faithfully for over a hundred years; a young boy shot dead on his way home from football practice.

On a memorable evening in May 2005, a huge number of Liverpool supporters felt themselves to be on a fragile boundary which rested in a sports stadium in Istanbul. Defeat or victory in the Champions League was held in balance to the very last moments of a penalty shoot-out. Liverpool won and the following evening three quarters of a million people turned out to greet the team bus as it drove through the streets from the airport to St George's Plateau. Over 300,000 people were packed into that space for hours. The street cleaners faced a litter mountain, but the police had a trouble-free exercise marred by only three arrests for minor offences.

The Twenty-Fifth River Festival Service was held in the parish church on 10 June 2005. To my delight the Rector, the Rev. Steven Brookes, asked me to assist him in the planning and writing of the service – in my mind it was a liturgical version of this book! Lord Lieutenant, Lord Mayor, High Sheriff and distinguished figures from the city formed the congregation which was seated in great semi-circles round a rowing boat in the centre of the church,. As the story of the city unfolded, three children brought various symbols and placed them in the boat: produce of the little agricultural community of King John's borough, sacks and bales from the transatlantic trade, chains taken from the wrists of a black man by a small white girl, tin-hat and the trappings of the Blitz, the refuse and squalor of strike-stricken Liverpool as well as the great plans for the future. There was no River Mersey hymn in any of my hymn books and so I wrote one, to be sung to the tune 'Finlandia', and accompanied by the Band of the Royal Marines, Portsmouth. With a group of members of the church, I walked along the waterfront late that night immensely proud to be part of this city. This place on the Mersey shore has been my home for the whole of my life. Whatever might happen on shore, the ebb and flow of the tides will reflect the sunlight as well as the storm cloud, and the ebb and flow of those tides will remain an unignorable influence on the life of the world-famous city on the Mersey shore.

Liverpool marches into the future: granddaughter Charlotte on her third birthday.
ELIZABETH KENNERLEY

The river rises high in lonely hills,
Bright as the dawn so shining, fresh and free.
Onward it flows with grime and human ills,
The journey onwards ever to the sea.
West to the sunset, pouring to the ocean,
With tide and wave and never-ending sea.

Life-giving flow and ever-running stream,
Shelter and food, support of city trade.
Source of our hope, inspirer of our dream.
Selfish we are and human life degrade.
Through the dark night the tide unceasing runs
And washes clean the errors we have made.

Spirit of God, upon the waters move,
Pouring for all your never ending love.
Wash clean our sins who ever break your law;
Spirit of healing, hov'ring like a dove.
Let storm clouds fade and roaring winds be still,
Through rays of sunset pour on us your love.

Further reading

P. Aughton, *Liverpool: A People's History* (1990; 2007)

T. Baines, *History of Liverpool* (1852)

R. Brooke, *Liverpool As It Was, 1775–1800* (1853)

S. Brown and P. de Figueiredo, *Religion and Place* (2008)

G. Chandler, *Liverpool* (1957)

G. Chandler, *Liverpool Under James I* (Town Books, 1603–25) (1960)

G. Chandler, *Liverpool Under Charles I* (Town Books 1625–49) (1965)

H. Channon, *A Portrait of Liverpool* (1970)

D. Charters, *Liverpool: The World in One City* (2003)

E. W. Cox, 'An Attempt to Discover the Plans for the Castle of Liverpool', *Transactions of the Historic Society of Lancashire and Cheshire* (1927)

M. Fletcher, *The Making of Liverpool* (2004)

F. Gibberd, *Metropolitan Cathedral of Christ the King, Liverpool* (1968)

C. Giles and B. Hawkins, *Storehouses of Empire, Liverpool's Historic Warehouses* (2004)

E. F. Greenwood (ed.), *The Ecology and Landscape Development, A History of the Mersey Basin* (1999)

R. Griffiths, *The History of the Royal and Ancient Park of Toxteth, Liverpool* (1907)

Olde Liverpoole and Its Charter (1907)

P. Healey, *The Liverpool Blue Coat School* (1995)

J. Hollinshead, *Liverpool in the Sixteenth Century* (2008)

J. Hoult, *West Derby, Old Swan and Wavertree* (1913)

Q. Hughes, *Seaport* (1993)

Q. Hughes, *Liverpool, City of Architecture* (1999)

F. E. Hyde, *Liverpool and the Mersey* (1971)

A. Jarvis and K. Smith (eds), *Albert Dock: Trade and Technology* (1999)

A. Johnson, *Merseyside's Secret Blitz Diary* (2005)

M. Kelly, *The Life and Times of Kitty Wilkinson* (2000)

P. A. Kennerley, *The Building of Liverpool Cathedral* (1991)

P. A. Kennerley and C. Wilkinson, *The Cathedral Church of Christ in Liverpool* (2003)

K. Layton-Jones and R. Lee, *Places of Health and Amusement* (2008)

D. Lewis, *The Churches of Liverpool* (2001)

Liverpool Culture Company – *Sea Liverpool: Maritime History of a Great Port* (2005)

Liverpool Heritage Bureau – *Buildings of Liverpool* (1978)

Littlebury Brothers – *New Illustrated Guide to Liverpool* (1902)

D. A. Macnaughton – *Roscoe of Liverpool* (1996)

A. McIntyre-Brown & G. Woodland – *Liverpool the First Thousand Years* (2001)

E. Midwinter – *Old Liverpool Old Liverpool* (1971)

J. Moore – *Underground Liverpool* (1998)

R. Muir – *A History of Liverpool* (1907)

S. Nicholson – *The Changing Face of Liverpool 1207–1727* (1981)

P. Parker – *Liverpool Docks Four Decades of Change* (2004)

B. Perrett – *Liverpool City at War* (1990)

N. Pevsner – The Buildings of England: South Lancashire (1969)

J. A. Picton – Memorials of Liverpool (1873)

M. Power – Liverpool Town Books 1649 – 1671 (1999)

J. Sharples – Liverpool (2004)

J. Sharples and J. Stonard, *Builton Commerce* (2008)

D. Sheppard – Steps Along Hope Street (2002)

J. Stonehouse – The Streets of Liverpool (1869)

J. A. Twemlow – Liverpool Town Books (1550–1571)) 1918

J. A. Twemlow – Liverpool Town Books (1572–1603) 1935

D. Whale – Lost Villages of Liverpool (1984)

P. H. Williams – Liverpolitana (1971)

C. Wilkinson – The Streets of Liverpool (1988)

C. Wilkinson – More Streets of Liverpool (1989)

G. Woodland and L. Baxter – Liverpool World Heritage City (2004)